HASHTAGS

From
Sunday

HASHTAGS

HASHTAGS

Social Media,

Politics and

Ethnicity in Nigeria

NWACHUKWU EGBUNIKE

Dedication

For
Mildred Obiageli Egbunike
(Anachelunwa, Ojinwayo)

ISBN: 978-978-55723-6-0

Published in Nigeria in 2018 by Narrative Landscape Press
under its Prima Imprint
9, Odunlami Street, Anthony Village, Lagos, Nigeria
07014522083, 09090554406 – 7
contact@narrativelandscape.com
www.narrativelandscape.com

A catalogue record for this book is available from
the National Library of Nigeria.

Cover Design and Layout by Shobola Ibukun
Author Image: Courtesy of Author
Printed by Nutech Print Services

CONTENTS

DEFINITION OF TERMS

#TrollCabal: an online network of Nigerian Twitter users who make mockery of the drama that characterises the country's political space. Employing satire, this non-confessional, non-political and non-ethnic virtual network also provides a non-violent and humorous counter-narrative.

Banter (bants): a humorous, playful and friendly exchange of witty remarks.

Blogosphere: an online network or community of writers and readers of blogs.

Blogotivist: an online or social media activist.

Fencism: An unusual political alignment of some Twitter users in Nigeria who do not manifest their support for any political party online but maintain an objective political opinion.

Netizen: citizen of the internet.

Overlord: a Nigerian Twitter user with large followership, agenda setters, news framers, experts on all matters, and final social arbiters whose views, judgments and solutions must always prevail.

Politico-twitterati: elite or influential tweeps who are interested in politics.

Tweep: Twitter person (user).

Tweet fights: when tweeps exchange words, argue or have a virtual brawl over an issue on Twitter.

Tweetsphere: an online network and/or community of twitter users.

Twitter Nigeria: the online community of active Twitter users in Nigeria.

Twitvilla: the virtual network of twitter users.

Voltron: a word used in Twitter Nigeria to describe uncritical and herd followers of political Twitter (overlords) influencers.

FOREWORD

When the Future Meets with the Present – on the Back of the Past

It is a rare book indeed that competently executes a rendezvous of future and past in the present and thus gives its readers a breathtaking panorama of the timelessness of human existence in a timely manner. *Hashtags: Social Media, Politics and Ethnicity in Nigeria* is one such volume that has built a bridge of comprehension across generations by exploring the socio-political atmosphere in the Nigerian online community, easily the most vibrant on the African continent. The book has competently achieved its task of providing a body of illuminating essays through which "the aspirations, hopes, angst, frustrations and intentions of Nigerian tweeps about politics, ethnicity, free speech, hate speech and political participation" can be better understood.

The essays in the volume have benefited from the author's participant observation and ethnographic immersion in the Nigerian social media space since 2004. It is not surprising, therefore, that the volume offers path-breaking insights of a richly empirical, clinically rigorous, and competently comparative nature into the workings of the Nigerian social media landscape on the very important issues of ethnic hate speech, politics, and matters relating to free speech. I find this book seminal in several senses, and at the same time a celebration of the quality of intellectual engagement of Nigeria's youth in the affairs of their country – and continent.

I begin my comments in this regard with a focus on the youthfulness of the author of this book. I do this not in ageist condescension but to further underscore the point that has not been lost on those of us who constantly engage Nigerian youth in intellectual and other enterprises: that, more than at any other time in Nigeria's political history, the current conjuncture is blessed with youth with the requisite knowledge and experience for constructing pathways of escape from the current depressing context in which their country finds itself onto a more elevating future of their dream.

A signifier of the author's admirable competencies in research and writing is to be found in his combination of traditional and cutting-edge methods with beautiful and arresting writing style that uses simple language to report and comment on complex matters in manners that explain rather than confuse. The appropriate combination of participant observation and online ethnography has yielded the mine of data and perspectives reported in the book's beautifully designed and readable pages.

This important book is set to impact positively on the theory, practice and policy content and context of social media not only in Nigeria but also in the rest of the African continent. I commend it as essential reading to all those in policy, practice and academia, among others, who are genuinely interested in enriching their understanding of, and engagement with social media – especially in regard to such issues critical to peace, security, justice and equity as politics, hate speech, and the contours of free speech in the media of the moment and of the future.

Adigun Agbaje, PhD.
Professor of Political Communication,
University of Ibadan, Ibadan, Nigeria.
June 2018.

INTRODUCTION

Nigeria plays host to a vivacious social media ecology. This is not surprising since out of an estimated population of 180 million people, 86,219,965 are internet users. Nigeria has an internet penetration of 46.1% which constitutes 2.5% of over 3.4 billion global internet users.[1] The top ten most visited sites by Nigerian netizens are: Google.com, Google.com.ng, Facebook.com, Yahoo.com, Youtube.com, Twitter.com, Jumia.com.ng, Linkedin.com, Nairaland.com and Instagram.com.[2] As at 2010, Facebook was the second most popular site on the internet after Google.[3] Facebook usage data shows that 7.1 million Nigerians use Facebook daily and 15 million use the platform each month.[4]

Similarly, Nigeria is Africa's most active country in political conversations on Twitter, followed by South Africa, Ethiopia, Burundi and Egypt. Hashtags in Nigeria have a huge following, on the continent and outside. In 2015 alone, #ChibokGirls generated over 145,000 geolocated Twitter mentions in Nigeria. #BringBackOurGirls trended for "an impressive 365 days—unfathomable amount of time considering the small life span of most campaigns."[5] Twitter has some merits that other social media platforms lack. The architecture of Twitter is designed for brevity and immediacy. With the 280-character limit (until November 2017, it was 140), tweeps are confined to the bare essentials. In the fast-changing world of headlines and breaking news, this has a tremendous impact; people are forced to stick to the point.

Hashtags: Social Media, Politics and Ethnicity in Nigeria is a product of my ethnographic immersion in social media for the past fourteen years. Online ethnography or netnography is the adoption of ethnographic methods to investigate communities and cultures that emerge from computer-mediated social relations.[6,7] Like all qualitative methods, netnography is interested in understanding the contextual nuances of a group of people and is thus able to explain their social, political or cultural characteristics.[8, 9]

Most of the essays in the book are my interventions based on my participant-observation of social media since 2004 and specifically Twitter, since 2009. These articles were written for various blogs—which served as a diary of sorts—based on socio-political topics and/or an explanation of the sub-culture of the social actors.

Twitter Nigeria is a vibrant virtual community of many Twitter users (tweeps). The silos of these tweeps vary depending on their affinity for a particular topic. Thus, there is literary twitter, political twitter, football twitter, and more. Although most of these clusters intersect—as is expected of any social interaction—nonetheless, each group possesses a distinct virtually mediated culture that defines their community.

Political twitter seems to be the most postulating cluster in Twitter Nigeria. The reasons are obvious considering that politics is an art that engages emotions.[10] Politics also remains a common topic that binds many Nigerians, cutting across different groups, with conversations uniting different tweeps who share ideas on other issues. The conversations—or lack of it—exhibit varying nuances based on the tweeps involved. The underlying motives for the vicious and divisive narrations can only be fully appreciated by someone who has been fully involved in the community and thus understands the currents.

Hashtags has three sections. The first section contains posts that gauged the pulse of Nigerian tweeps on incendiary ethnic hate speech in the country. The second section contains essays that capture the political twitter community—showing partisan and non-partisan political alignments. Also, this section examines the evolution and underlying philosophy of the #TrollCabal, an online social experiment that caricatures the bile associated with political conversations. The last section features articles on online free speech, either as advocacy against gagged voices or a conceptual analysis of what free speech really means. The appendix contains two statements which I initiated based on the prevailing socio-political situation in Nigeria at the time. The first is a statement by concerned Nigerian bloggers calling for the immediate release of the abducted school girls from Chibok. The second was a statement by a group of Nigerian writers on the prevailing ethnocentric hate speech that threatened the corporate existence of the country. Both statements are reproduced here, both for posterity and to provide the context for some of the posts in the book.

Hashtags hopes to provide a glimpse into the nature of the socio-political atmosphere of Africa's most vibrant online politico-social ecosystem. Through this collection of essays, the aspirations, hopes, angst, frustrations and intentions of Nigerian tweeps about politics, ethnicity, free speech, hate speech and political participation can be better understood.

PART I
ETHNIC HATE SPEECH

NIGERIA: CURBING THE TIDE
OF ETHNIC HATE–ONLINE AND OFFLINE

The right of citizens to talk, to express opinions and to keep tabs on governance is an inherent aspect of any democratic culture. However, conversation spaces have long expanded beyond pubs and other physical spheres to include digitally mediated online public spaces. A 2016 report: *How Africa Tweets* states that by the volume of geo-located tweets, Nigeria, is the most active African country for political conversations on Twitter, followed by South Africa, Ethiopia, Burundi and Egypt. Our vibrant digital sphere, however, is fraught with hatred and vile speech. A good portion of the hate speech in Nigeria is ethno-religious in nature. With over two hundred and fifty ethnic groups and five hundred languages, the country has a history of conflicts dating back, to 1914, when Great Britain joined the colonial territories of Southern and Northern Nigeria to create a single state.

Ethno-religious conflict continued to bedevil the nation after independence in 1960. Successive administrations in the country for selfish reasons employed ethno-religious sentiments to shore up their support base. However, the draconian laws suppressing free speech and association during decades of military dictatorship kept the situation relatively in check. It was the peace of a graveyard. The twenty-eight-year military intervention in fact, aggravated the ethnic divide by bringing ethnic rivalry to the forefront of national life. Everything was viewed from the prism of "us" versus "them". Nigerians were thus hopeful with the return of democracy in 1999. The ethnic tensions that had characterised the country's politics—especially with the annulment of the 12 June 1993 presidential elections by General Ibrahim Babangida, and the truncated self-succession attempt by late General Sani Abacha—seemed to have been neutralised by the election of President Olusegun Obasanjo. The national mood at that time appeared to be a fulfilment of some part of the old National Anthem: "Though tribe and tongue may differ, in brotherhood we stand." Sadly, this hope was short-lived. The spectre of ethnic rivalry was resuscitated with the constitution of the Human Rights Violation Commission, also called the Oputa Panel, through which different ethnic groups sought justice for perceived crimes against them. The macabre tales that flowed from the various petitions showed that the old wounds and bottled-up grievances were far from healed. The reconciliation sought by the Oputa Panel was never achieved because institutional confrontation of our searing national memory was neither in the agenda of the political actors nor their political parties.

Party politics in Nigeria has no ideological foundation. A lust for power and looting the public till is the only unifying factor. Thus, civilians who have aided the military, retired soldiers and their cronies, continue to dominate party politics. This makes the problem of ethnic conflict even more intractable, as those who wield power have a vested interest in maintaining the status quo.

For social media and its influence on Nigerian politics, the turning point was the 2015 presidential elections. Digital media asserted itself as the new medium of choice for political parties seeking to influence public opinion and canvass for votes. While social media may not yet be a primary factor in determining election outcomes or propelling electoral campaigns, almost half of Nigeria's population[11] now have internet access, and for the 18-35 age group, social media plays a major role in influencing political choices.[12] Just like any communication tool, the internet can be the purveyor of both the good and the ugly. It has also been shown to be a kind of "echo chamber", a space where individuals connect and associate primarily with people with similar opinions to theirs. The influence of Nigerian online "overlords", who can influence the opinions and actions of their numerous followers regarding topical issues, has transformed social media into an effective amplifier of hate speech, and the ability for users to remain anonymous exacerbates this.

Ethnocentrism flourished on social networks, after the release of the 2015 presidential election results. A study[13] which I participated in, did a content analysis of two hundred and fifty tweets bearing the #Igbo hashtag, referring to the Igbo people of south-eastern Nigeria. The findings were alarming. We found a prevalence of derogatory, mocking tweets blaming one ethnic group for not voting President Muhammadu Buhari. The findings were reinforced by the official results released by the national electoral umpire, which showed that voting in the 2015 elections occurred along ethnic lines.

President Buhari won the 2015 presidential elections with over 3 million votes[14] to beat incumbent, Dr Goodluck Jonathan. Buhari's All Peoples Congress (APC) is a coalition of politicians from the north and south-western parts of Nigeria. Thus, it was "normal" within the context of Nigeria's parochial politics that Buhari got a majority of his votes from most of the north and south-west. The south-west is the ethnic base of Buhari's chief collaborator and party leader, Bola Tinubu and also of Buhari's deputy, Yemi Osinbajo. On the other hand, Jonathan got block votes from the south-south and south-east parts of the country. Although Jonathan is from the south-south, the south-east had adopted him as "our son" because of close ethnic proximity. Consequently, it was a done deal when APC won in North-Central, North-East, North-West and South-West regions. Same goes with PDP that won in the South-East and South-South Zones.

Nonetheless, Nigeria is hardly the only country in the world where ethnic divisions appear to be deepening. In 2016, the US grappled with the most decisive presidential election in the country's history, in which one of the candidates turned hate into a weapon for canvassing votes. Guess what? He won. The UK's #Brexit referendum in June 2017 was alleged to have been propelled by the bitterness of some Britons with regard to immigration. And here on the African continent, ethnocentric hatred was instrumental in the 2007 violent post-election clashes in Kenya which were propagated largely through digital technology, particularly SMS.

The essence of participatory democracy, however, means that preserving the right to freedom of speech online is incontestable. This becomes even more important because the online space on the African continent is already jeopardised by government interference—the detention of a pro-government blogger[15] in Nigeria; the assault on digital media in Ethiopia[16]; the imprisonment of dissidents in the Gambia[17] during former President Yahya Jammeh's regime; the imposed social media blackout during the 2016 Ugandan elections[18]; and the moves by the governments of Uganda and Nigeria in 2016 to impose stricter controls for social media[19] demonstrate the lengths to which states will go to suppress free expression in the online space.

We cannot afford to self-immolate or hand our rights over to hawks looking for any excuse to subvert free speech, either online or offline. But Nigerians also need to guard against the hijack of public conversation by forces that promote division.

A practical solution would be to adopt the report of the

2014 National Conference (#NGConfab). As imperfect as it is, one of the recommendations of the #NGConfab was the rotation of the office of President between the North and South through the country's six geo-political zones (North East, North West, North Central, South East, South West and South-South). It is time we dump the hypocritical sophistication of running an ideologically driven politics to accept that ours is basically an ethno-religious power sharing. There is no reason to keep the pretence that our politicians will ever be interested in pursuing common good at the expense of their greed for power and the tills of office. In order to limit the continual cycle of ethnic hate as a weapon of pursuing or maintaining political office, let each region take a turn at the presidency in an orderly fashion. This institutionalisation of *the turn-by-turn, chop-I-chop* rotational presidency will be Nigeria's greatest contribution to the global evolution of political systems of government. In that way, agency will be taken away from those who profit from stoking ethno-religious conflict through politics. Consequently, an arrangement like this could go a long way toward curbing the tide of ethnic hate and its attendant bile, in political conversation—both online and offline—in Nigeria.

Global Voices
29 August 2016

ETHNIC HATE SPEECH, NIGERIAN WRITERS AND SOCIAL MEDIA

The marauding butcher militant group, Boko Haram, is still devouring Nigeria, but Africa's most populous nation is under another intense strain of the most virulent type—ethnic hate speech. Things have deteriorated so badly that fears of another ethnic war in Nigeria are rapidly rising.

On 28 June 2017, twenty-seven Nigerian writers, concerned about the escalating tensions from different ethnic groups in the country, released a public statement condemning this rising trend of ethnocentric hate speech (*see Appendix 2*). Some of the writers include me, Tade Ipadeola (poet and winner of the 2013 Nigeria Prize for Literature), Kola Tubosun (writer and linguist), Ikhide Ikheloa (writer and critic), Chika Unigwe, (multiple award-winning novelist), Abubakar Adam Ibrahim (novelist and winner of the 2016 Nigeria Prize for Literature), Eghosa Imasuen (novelist and publisher), Temitayo Olofinlua (writer and communication scholar), amongst others. The statement reads thus:

We, the undersigned Nigerian writers, view with grave concern the dominance of ethnic incendiary speech in our country. We are deeply troubled that the public space—both online and offline—has been hijacked by a vocal minority of individuals who promote ethnocentric ideas inimitable to the peace and well-being of a majority of citizens. Nigerian citizens have a right to freely express their opinions on governance as enshrined in the Constitution. However, this fundamental right of freedom of speech is being used to disseminate hate speech, which goes contrary to the right itself and the spirit of the Constitution that enshrines it…

The "us" against "them" rhetoric that has ignited bloodshed of a bestial magnitude since independence has re-surfaced again. A new breed of ethnic entrepreneurs seems hell-bent on causing anarchy for political motives. The lessons of our history are being ignored. Strength in diversity is considered weakness… We strongly believe that no amount of social grievance against the government can justify this level of irresponsible ethnocentric hatred currently being peddled by a growing number of disgruntled groups in this country. Similarly, we are mortified by the initial nonchalance and apparent misguided handling by the authorities of the root cause of hate speech in the country.

It is important to state that hate speeches, for the most part of 2017, came from multiple factions. One troubling example emanates from the south-eastern part of the country, where Nnamdi Kanu, leader of the Indigenous People of Biafra (IPOB), converted Radio Biafra into a tool that, not only facilitated political mobilisation for secession from the Nigerian state, but was also used as a platform for spewing hate speeches[20] directed at his opponents.

Radio Biafra broadcasts have been characterised as toxic rhetoric aimed at other ethnic groups in Nigeria. The station described the country as a "zoo" that the IPOB intends to "destroy". However, Kanu claimed that his reference to Nigeria as a zoo was "to facilitate societal change"[21, 22].

Nigerian blogger, Kemisola Adeyemi, quoted a listener from a call-in radio show on the radio station, actively offering to carry out violent tactics against other ethnic groups:

> *A caller said he was a technician of sorts and was willing to offer his services to help build a bomb to destroy Nigeria, and the Nnamdi character took his number and promised to get in touch with him. The calls kept coming in and it was just caller after caller pledging support for the cause of this deranged man. It didn't matter that the Nnamdi character sounded rude, arrogant and full of himself and obviously had a thirst for power, it didn't matter that he was insulting and disrespecting most of the callers who dialled [sic] in, more people kept calling...I couldn't help but*

remember that this was exactly how the Boko Haram menace started. First it was just an Islamic preacher who was also doing charity works and feeding his followers, then it grew into a militia that has caused the death of over 15,000 Nigerians and counting... [23]

The listener continued, pleading with state authorities to assert control over the situation before "innocent lives" are lost.

Sectarianism and Ethnicity: Fatal Poisons

With over five hundred ethnic groups and about two hundred and fifty languages, ethnocentric violence has bedevilled the West African nation since Independence. The 28-year military dictatorship in the country suppressed free speech and exacerbated ethnic divide. Thus, everything was viewed from the prism of "us" versus "them". The Nigerian state is complicit in creating the environment for messages like Kanu's to fester. President Muhammadu Buhari in an address at the United States Institute of Peace (USIP) in July 2016 said that he would not run an inclusive government because "the constituents, for example, gave me 97% [of the votes] and cannot in all honesty be treated on some issues with constituencies that gave me 5%." [24]

This statement was lived out to the fullest extent. Thus, it was not surprising when *Punch Newspapers* denounced President Buhari's "parochial appointments" in a 1 August 2016 editorial:

> *Buhari's sectionalism is not only unprecedented; it could not have come at a worse time. The reality today is that Nigerians are deeply divided. Seventeen years of dashed hopes of progress under a democratic dispensation have reopened the deep fissures in the polity and polarised the populace into mutually suspicious camps. Sectarianism and ethnicity have been rearing their poisonous heads.*[25]

Other factions have added to this divisive ethnic politics and attendant hate speech in the country. Some northern youths in a statement entitled the "Kaduna Declaration" gave the Igbos three months' notice to quit northern Nigeria:

> *As a first step, since the Igbo have clearly abused the unreciprocated hospitality that gave them unrestricted access to, and ownership of landed properties all over the North, our first major move shall be to reclaim, assume and assert sole ownership and control of these landed resources currently owned, rented or in any way enjoyed by the ingrate Igbos in any part of Northern Nigeria... Secondly, with the effective date of this declaration, which is today, Tuesday, June 06, 2017, all Igbos currently residing in any part of Northern*

Nigeria are hereby served notice to relocate within three months and all northerners residing in the East are advised likewise.[26]

This incendiary document from the northern youths to the Igbos drew the ire of those from the oil-rich Niger Delta of Nigeria. They described the statement as "tragic and more treasonable than the offence allegedly committed by Nnamdi Kanu, leader of IPOB, for which he was held in detention for about a year."[27] Kanu, who was arrested in 2015 on an 11-count charge of terrorism and treasonable felony, was later granted bail.

The confusion was heightened by President Buhari's absence, as he had left for a fresh round of medical treatment at the British capital on 7 May and had not been heard from, or seen, since then. His deputy, Professor Yemi Osinbajo, who had been acting in his stead, was consulting with various representatives of ethnic groups in the country. However, the acting president was urged to expand his consultations from the moderate representatives of ethnic groups to those deifying the ethnic champions.

These and many other inflammatory remarks moved Nigerian writers to sound the alarm on ethnocentric hate speech and to urge the government to act and prevent possible ethnic violence in their country:

We also call on the government of Nigeria to do everything in its power to protect her citizens and avert another spate of useless killings, and to listen to all aggrieved segments in a constructive and productive manner. It is the duty of government to make the country livable, just as it is for citizens to work on building a country to which we are all happy to belong. This means an interrogation of our national memory, reinstating the teaching of a thorough curriculum of Nigerian history in primary and secondary schools, a celebration of our individual cultures and languages, and, above all, the application of justice where rights have been violated.

Global Voices
12 July 2017

OLD SENTIMENTS, NEW TOOLS

Nigeria fought a bitter civil war from 1967 to 1970. This conflict was fuelled, amongst many other reasons, by political events that sowed deep suspicion rooted in ethnic differences between the principal Nigerian political actors of the First Republic. While the real reasons behind the conflict that led to the death of over a hundred thousand military causalities and an estimated one million Biafran civilian deaths is shrouded in official secrecy, the historical import of this war continues to be told from the bias of each side.

However, the effect of the war continues to haunt the country. This is obviously expected considering the horrors of bestial proportions that preceded and occurred during the conflict. One of the triggers of the civil war was the reported massacres of Igbos by their Hausa hosts in Kano. Heerteen and Moses[28] explain:

> Repeated outbursts of violence between June and October 1966 peaked in massacres against Igbos living in the Sabon Gari, the "foreigners' quarters" of northern Nigerian towns. According to estimates, these riots claimed the lives of tens of thousands. This

violence drove a stream of more than a million refugees to the Eastern Region, the "homeland" of the Igbos' diasporic community (Heerten & Moses, 2014, p. 173).

The killings in the north led to the fleeing of Igbos back to the eastern region and the retaliatory expelling of non-Igbos from the East. The Nigerian-Biafran civil war had started. However, this was Nigeria of 1970s with no social media. With hands now always typing on phones communicating with the rest of the world, the memory of the Nigeria civil war became incarnated in the twenty-first century. The only difference is that the principal actors had changed but the conversations are the same. Unfortunately, the historical nuanced context imperative of the long-old ethnic conflicts between the Hausa and Igbo was totally absent. This explains the grave motivation that impelled Nigerian writers to make that public statement.

Netizens, Ethnicity and Ethnic Hate Speech in Nigeria

Nigeria is an ethnic fault-line state with different ethnic nationalities obstinately holding on to their prejudices. Yet, the question remains if social media exposure, immersion or use broadened the users' ethnic perception, making it more accommodating or tolerant? Or has it restricted it, making no difference or even deepening the ethnic stereotypes?

Ethnic cleavages have morphed into defining identity for many Nigerian citizens. In the absence of a strong national identity, the primordial ethnic identities reign supreme. Thus, Osaghae and Suberu assert that: "ethnicity is generally regarded as the most basic and politically salient identity in Nigeria. This claim is supported by the fact that both in competitive and non-competitive settings, Nigerians are more likely to define themselves in terms of their ethnic affinities than any other identity."[29]

On the other hand, Nigeria is a country with an intimidating youthful population. This demographic of digital natives use social media as their conversational space. This is both the media and the network for them. These young Nigerian netizens are ever ready to express their enormous popular dissatisfaction, frustration and mistrust. Since many of them were not taught history as a subject in secondary school, most of them lack the critical perspective to evaluate political stories from the past.

All they see around them are broken promises and crushed hopes. Some of these netizens are trying to figure out how to build political movements that are positive, forward-looking and non-ethnic. But they soon realise that sadly their hopes may never rise in Nigeria. In situations like this, they talk using the only media they know and have – digital media. Some of these frustrated netizens inadvertently employ digital media to amplify ethnocentric hate speech.

The role of influencers on Nigerian social media ecology, particularly Twitter, is essential in understanding how social media becomes an enabler of hate speech. In Twitter Nigeria, the influencers (overlords) command great followership. These overlords also maintain a certain hold on their followers (voltrons) who in turn almost idolise their overlords with the cult of divine worship. Thus, the fanatical frenzy of voltrons to always be on the same page with their overlords is a given especially when it comes to political issues. In this situation, it is not surprising that an overlord becomes the instigator of ethnic hate speech which is sheepishly propagated, and even defended by their voltrons. This was the case for instance, in the aftermath of the 2015 presidential elections.[30]

Unfortunately, most voltrons do not realise that their overlords are hired hirelings of politicians—mere tools for the propagation of outright falsehoods. In the build up to the 2015 presidential elections, some of these overlords who had built up an activist social media persona during the 2012 #OccupyNigeria protests became megaphones for politicians and/or political parties. They were therefore able to frame the narrative against the ruling government through a militant amplification of gaffes and incompetence. This overtime validated their activist credentials. Sadly, the entire frustration with the system coupled with an absence of history only escalates the news dependency of voltrons on the frames pushed out by their overlords. With time, some of these overlords simply morphed into hate speech propagators.[31]

However, these traits are not exclusive to Twitter Nigeria but are also present in the political storytelling on Facebook. In a 2016 study[32], respondents identified five themes as drivers of ethnicity on their friends' Facebook walls as bias, tribalism, marginalisation, bigotry and subjectivity. These netizens had no inhibition in pointing out the ethnic bias of their Facebook friends – "others" – political narration but absolved themselves of any blame. This is often the case when describing other people's display of ethnic hate while turning a blind eye to oneself. On the other hand, Facebook storytelling was a mixed bag of the good and ugly. There were positive connotations that showed that Facebook was useful medium for freedom of expression and ethnic integration. Similarly, there hate speech, divisive ethnic posts, trolling/cyber bullying using ethnic slurs and stereotypes were also rife. The verdict of the study was that the political storytelling on Facebook aided ethnic divisions.

Like a double-edged sword, while social media may be a good tool for information dissemination, it could also be a purveyor of hate speech. Many people are unable to identify what side of the sword is being used, they only take the sword and continue its use. This could have dire consequences for not just individuals but nations.

SURPRISE SPEECH: MR PRESIDENT'S HEALTH AND ETHNIC TENSIONS

President Muhammadu Buhari is back in Nigeria after a three-month-long unexplained "medical vacation"[33] in the UK. In his first national broadcast since his return 48 hours later, he did not talk about his personal health or healthcare in the country. Instead, he addressed divisive ethnic-politics. He remarked that while he was away, he was "distressed to see comments in social media discussions about current affairs that crossed our national red lines by daring to question our collective existence as a nation." He continued:

> *Nigeria's unity is settled and not negotiable. We shall not allow irresponsible elements to start trouble and when things get bad they run away and saddle others with the responsibility of bringing back order, if necessary with their blood. Every Nigerian has the right to live and pursue his business anywhere in Nigeria without let or hindrance. I believe the very vast majority of Nigerians share this view. This is not to deny that there are legitimate concerns. Every group has a grievance. But the beauty and attraction of a federation is that it allows different groups to air their grievances and work out a mode of co-existence.[34]*

21

Ethnic hate speeches online have been on the rise since the 2015 presidential elections in the country. Recently, from the south-east of the country, the Indigenous People of Biafra (IPOB) led by Nnamdi Kanu has been clamouring for secession from Nigeria. This precipitated a series of events, chief among which was the "Kaduna Declaration" a notice published by a group of northern youths giving any people of the Igbo ethnicity three months to leave Northern Nigeria.

In his speech, the president gave no official pronouncement on the state of his health. Although many Nigerians are glad to have the commander-in-chief back home, that fact did not go unnoticed. The lack of transparency over what ails Buhari has been a source of public speculation. Nigerians had hoped that the president would have used the opportunity of the broadcast to refute the rumours about his health. We were disappointed. Buhari said nothing about his sickness. Nonetheless, his speech on ethnic tensions drew mixed reactions from Nigerians. Dr Oby Ezekwesili, a former minister and leader of the Bring Back Our Girls campaign, tweeted:

Oby Ezekwesili (@obyezeks), "I can give an instant citizen's feedback to President @MBuhari that his speech this morning was a terrible case of MISSED OPPORTUNITY," 21 August 2017, 8:37 a.m., https://twitter.com/obyezeks/status/

Patrick Okigbo III, in a Facebook post, was also not happy with the tone of the presidential broadcast:

> *I am a Nigerian, pure and simple, but I do not agree that "Nigeria's unity has been settled and is not negotiable". That would be bondage and not based on freewill. [...] I believe that we are better and stronger together. However, I believe that every group must be strong to come to a common table to negotiate their space. The role of the Federal Government is to make it possible for this dialogue to happen within a safe space. We must engage the various ethnic nationalities and figure out how best to create a nation that works for all. Banging on the table and proclaiming a non-negotiable union can work for a time and then the seams will give way. The sound you hear in the south-east today is the ripping apart of the weakened thread. Nnamdi Kanu's movement is not a joke. It is not a bad hangover that will go away. Rather, it is an opportunity for Nigeria to put a number of issues on the table and rigorously engage them. As they say, the best time to plant that tree was twenty years ago; the next best time is now. Taa ka bu gbo. Today is still a good enough time to start.[35]*

Nnamdi Kanu was arrested in 2015 on an 11-count charge of terrorism and treasonable felony and was granted bail in

2017. Some think the government's decision to prosecute him might have worsened an already dangerous situation. Media commentator, Dr Reuben Abati wrote:

> *Fifty years after the outbreak of the Civil War, we now have a man called Nnamdi Kanu. He may well end up as Nigeria's nemesis. He is the most frightening product of our many years and acts of denial and he may well throw the country into a nightmare worse than Boko Haram, if care is not taken… He and those who bought into his rhetoric of secession and the renewal of the Biafran dream organised protests across the world, and they looked, from afar, like a group of disgruntled Nigerians in diaspora. […] Whoever ordered Nnamdi Kanu's arrest and prosecution did this country a bad turn. Kanu is a character that could have been better ignored. His trial and travails have turned him into a hero and a living martyr among Igbos. And the young man so far, understands the game. Since he was released on bail, he has been taunting the Nigerian state and government.*[36]

However, there were Nigerians who supported President Buhari's speech. Nigerian poet Ikeogu Oke shared this on his Facebook wall:

> *I have read—and reread—the latest speech by President Buhari. I agree that it could be improved,*

like any other speech. But I'm surprised that one of the strictures against it is that it says Nigeria's unity is not negotiable. Did anyone in their right senses expect Buhari or the leader of any other country to openly declare in a national broadcast that the country's unity is negotiable, thereby sanctioning agitations for its breakup? Can anyone point to a precedent where any leader formally pronounced the unity of their country negotiable, even in the so-called civilised world? Even if such a precedent were to exist, are the underlying circumstances the same as ours? [...] As for me, I agree that the unity of any nation ought to be negotiable. But to expect any leader to proclaim that in a national broadcast is to take an unreasonable expectation too far.[37]

Nigerian writer, Mazi Nwonwu summarised the hostile ethnic politics in Nigeria first by taking a look at Nigerian literature, and then analysing the commentators on articles about the sitting president. He notes that the comments reflect ethnic leanings and portray a reality from a previous time in Nigerian history:

Did any of you read 'Divided We Stand' by the gifted Ekwensi? It is a forerunner of Chimamanda Ngozi Adichie's cerebral 'Half of a Yellow Sun'. Both books share many things in common, but the most striking is demonstrating that even in the midst of the turmoil before the war and the war proper, many northerners, easterners and westerners navigated their relationships and found a way to be together. But…this is not about the books or the brilliant writers behind them. This is about how we seem to stand divided and how this division is exemplified by how we view issues. So, someone writes something beautiful against our sitting president; you would most likely find names like Obi, Chima, Ngozi, etc., hailing the writer and his craft and superb brain. Another writes something pro-Buhari that's considered equally beautiful and you'd find the Adamus and Sanis hailing. In the midst of all this, is the Yinkas and Salawus who remain… in the middle, echoes of their fathers before them. It's funny, but both books captured this mode from that time our fathers thought they won't revisit. More than four decades later, we are here again, clinging to the same lines drawn in the sand by yesterday.[38]

Nigeria has been bedevilled by ethnic politics since independence in 1960. In the words of these two scholars, Felicia H. Ayatse and Isaac Iorhen Akuva: "Nigeria has carried forward the spirit of ethnicity into the postcolonial Nigeria, this vice has been discovered to have been responsible for most of the political, administrative, economic, social and cultural maladies in Nigeria."[39] Sadly, these sentiments have been exploited by most Nigerian politicians till date.

Global Voices
29 August 2017

Postscript

Nnamdi Kanu after he was granted bail in 2017 was supposed to keep to his house and not grant any public interview. However, Kanu broke all these conditions by visiting many towns outside Umuahia where he was residing in his father's house. Not only that, he granted many interviews to international media and did not cease his divisive ethnocentric rhetoric. Things came to a head with his organisation IPOB stating that there should be no governorship elections in Anambra state. The federal government reacted by declaring IPOB a terrorist organisation and launching a military operation in south-east Nigeria called *Operation Python Dance*. The military invaded Kanu's father's home and since then Kanu has neither been seen nor heard from.

Nigerian social media reacted to all these events in similar fashion – a bitter bifurcated conversation. The crux of which has been explained in the preceding chapter. However, since this statement by the president on the ethnic tensions and his health had political undertones, the reactions were also based on the partisan allegiances on Twitter. The varying political bias of tweeps will be the focus of the next section.

PART II

POLITICS, SOCIAL MEDIA AND THE
NIGERIAN POLITICO-TWITTERATI

FACEBOOKING: FROM VIRTUAL TO VISUAL

Chuka and I were classmates at Dennis Memorial Grammar School, Onitsha. Upon passing out, we parted ways shortly only to meet again at the university. Almost a decade after graduation, Chuka requested to be friends with me on Facebook. Unfortunately, I gave him a hell of a time while trying to prove his identity. Since I lack the gift of matching people's faces with the place where we first met, I had a bit of difficulty remembering him.

With a great deal of patience, he helped me recall the location of our first acquaintance. Then we got "chatting" only to realise that he works in Ife, a two-hour drive from Ibadan. This virtual friendship continued until we jumped out of cyberspace into reality. I finally met this childhood friend, who also happens to run a business in Ibadan. We have been hanging out since then, reliving old times and looking into the future.

People have different experiences on social networking sites. For many like me, Facebook is not only a utility to network; it's one of the best inventions of our time. This is a network that enables "storytelling" and gives one an opportunity to "friend or not to friend" (in Chi

Chi Layor's words). Asides that, I see it as a village square where there is perpetual activity, during the day and at night.

However, like all media, Facebook can be a waste of time. There is the inherent temptation to peer into other people's lives, to look up their photographs and read the latest gossips. Nonetheless, one cannot but admit that it is also a great tool for virtual mediated interpersonal communication. Little wonder that politicians seek to engage the audience that it serves.

While I have no intention of either beatifying or demonising Facebook, I would rather say that, for me, it has been a tremendous asset. Besides providing the platform to catch up with long forgotten friends and reminisce over the past, it is an influential means of communication which no one can easily ignore.

Feathers Project
29 October 2010

Postscript

Facebook compromised the privacy of her users by allowing personal information to be mined by Cambridge Analytica for election purposes in various parts of the world. This is obviously a very sad development for a tech company that claims to hold its users in great esteem. It also brings up many questions as regards online privacy and surveillance, especially in a country like ours where personal data is collected for different purposes and from various sources. What happens to the biometrics details collected during registration for BVN, vehicle license, national identity card, national passport, SIM card and others? Who stores them and where? How come same details are constantly received by various agencies with no central co-ordination? How sure are we that our personal details will not be employed by agents of the state to impede on our human rights to privacy? Or sold to a third party for commercial purposes? If these are the questions, what then are the answers?

SOCIAL MEDIA: POLITICAL FLAME
OR DAMP SQUIB?

The online virus was what globalised Tunisia's "Jasmine" revolution and sent Zine El Abidine Ben Ali packing. While this has been seen as a universal convergence against dictatorships, it may also have signalled a spike in the political power of social media. Observers wonder: can social media ignite a similar democratic flame in Nigeria or will it be a damp squib?

2011 Elections and the Social Media

The political space in the country has been broadened by the hyperactivity of young people who not only desire change but are impatient about it. With the influx of many groups with a dominating online presence, the 2011 elections seem to be too important to be left for politicians alone. Familiar names like "Vote or Quench", "RSVP (Register, Select, Vote and Protect)", and "If Naija Votes", have assumed buzz status. More importantly is that a crowd of young Nigerians are making it trendy. As at January 2011, Facebook had 2,777,440 registered Nigerians—ranking it 38 out of 213 countries.

The digital media is a blanket term for the internet

and mobile telephony. A hybrid of video, text messaging and audio information all available on the internet, the social media is a subgroup of digital media; providing an interactive platform for online communities to share information. Chief amongst these are e-mails, text messages, Twitter, Facebook, LinkedIn, and more.

Asides early adopters like Patrick Utomi and Nuhu Ribadu, other top Nigerian politicians are becoming more and more internet savvy. Jonathan Goodluck not only hugged Facebook but declared his presidential ambition on that platform and made a book – *My Friends and I* – from his conversations with his Facebook friends. Soon after, Ibrahim Badamosi Babangida, former military head of state; Atiku Abubakar, then vice president and Godswill Akpabio, the former governor of Akwa Ibom state, followed suit.

Besides politicians, social media was also used to monitor INEC voters' registration. Citizens came online and tweeted at the electoral body on the different challenges they experienced while trying to register. The predominance of tweets with #inecregistration also attests to this. Also, the Delta State 2011 run-off election was observed via Twitter and Facebook. The PDP presidential election was a global trending topic on Twitter—with the contestants and Nigeria rebranded through the cyber gaze.

Down with Gatekeepers!

The once cultish aura of traditional media (TV, radio, newspaper and other print media) has been broken. With internet freedom, there is no longer a clear distinction between the news consumers and news creators. Clay Shirky in his Foreign Affairs essay "The Political Power of Social Media" conceptualised internet freedom as outlined by the US Secretary of State, Hillary Clinton. This freedom comprises of three essential ingredients: "freedom to access information, freedom of ordinary citizens to produce their own public media; and freedom of citizens to converse with one another."[40]

The ubiquity of social media makes it more difficult to track. One thing is obvious: people are talking, not only within the rigid milieu of localisation, but beyond it. Armed with a smart phone, more Nigerians now have access to information and thus spill the bile they have bottled up for so long. The greatest weapon of this century seems to have shifted from the gun to the connected mobile phone.

With a reckless political oligarchy flaunting corruption as a norm, the economic curve of the Nigerian situation makes online "clicking" quite attractive. Majority of these young Nigerians asides being eligible to vote, also bear personal scars of the mismanagement of our commonwealth. They want a "better life" for their children. They desire constant electricity supply. They want better jobs. They want suitable homes. In short, they desire a more dignifying future. This is the group that has ignited the political flame via social media. Their vocal outburst is a manifestation of a deep-seated pain. What is not yet certain is whether this flame will continue to burn or fizzle out.

Prophet or Pathologist?

Prophets have the divine ability to peer into the future while pathologists are sages made wise by hindsight. Though my ability to foresee lacks any divine potential, I think I am quite comfortable prophesying a rise in the political power of social media in Nigeria. The traits are quite obvious. By the way, most Nigerian prophets deserve a first-class ticket to the infernal pit for manipulating poverty for fantasy. And I hereby separate myself from that class of prophets.

The legitimacy of conversations on these current media platforms show that it will endure. This is far from the flimsy flippancy common among teenagers; this is a real-life situation! Having said this, I concur with Clay Shirky that, "A public sphere is more likely to emerge in a society as a result of people's dissatisfaction with matters of economics or day-to-day governance, than from their embrace of abstract political ideals."[41] It is true that not all who join the conversation will translate their courage online to real life. Yet, if only twenty percent (555, 488) of the Facebook Nigerian population actually RSVP

(Register, Select, Vote and Protect), it will take more than rigging to beat that.

However, there are the usual early teething challenges concerning social media use for political participation. A friend lamented the lack of synchronisation (without hashtags) of tweets during the Delta run-off election. I encountered the same bump when trying to do a blog post on INEC registration in my area in Ibadan. It was difficult to classify information based on city, area and then, wards. Nonetheless, this is a minor hitch that I hope will be easily resolved, because a preponderance of information without order is useless.

For those still expecting a revolution, the truth is that we are already witnessing one. While it makes sense to rant about cleaning up the slate, the truth is that, that kind of violence never solves anything but creates more problems. With the click of a button, messages go viral from our various digital devices. Quietly but effectively, this is effecting the change we all dream of. May the political fire of the social media endure and not fade.

Feathers Project
25 January 2011

THE NIGERIAN TWITTERATI: SAINTS AND SINNERS?

In the past days, Twitter was turned into a battle field: an arena for spiteful exchanges between two groups of "respected" young Nigerian opinion leaders. What was the crux of the fight? One of them—who works for the government—had insulted the other group. What followed was an exchange of ad hominem tweets from the offended group and their followers. I am not concerned about the pettiness of that act and I do not intend to join the conversation, for or against. However, this incident ruptured a latent but deadly metastasis that is gradually characterising the Nigerian Twitter crowd. The twitter public sphere seems to be divided between saints and sinners.

Using the frame conceptualisation, an over-simplification, the saintly Nigerian Twitter elite is one who always criticises government and her agents. The saintly twitter elite could also be one who has at some point engaged in government services and has an unrepentant bias against netizens. On the other hand, the twitter sinner is one who has done the unpardonable; taken up a government appointment, never lashes out at government, and sees only good from that sector.

This same over-simplification was evident in the framing of the Arab Spring, the initial reaction, which still persists in some quarters, was that of a Twitter or Facebook revolution. This assumption did not stand the test of evidence which shows that although social media played a great role in the revolt in Egypt, it was demeaning to label it a Twitter or Facebook revolution. Rather, it took an intricate synergy of traditional, digital media and human involvement to get Mubarak packing. In my own view, both camps, saints and sinners, are wrong! This bifurcation is hinged on generalisations that may have no basis in reality. For the establishment crowd, all critics are necessarily noisemakers seeking attention, only waiting to be bought over to perpetual silence or praise singing. It is also not always true that anyone who crosses over to the "dark side" of government has lost their soul and automatically won a lottery ticket to be maligned.

No doubt, there will always be instances that would seem to justify both stances, the list is endless. However, to fall into the same pitfall that has characterised the Nigerian public space by the so-called "future of our country" is indeed pathetic. In righteous indignation, we all cringed at the public vitriolic between Obasanjo and Babangida in August 2011; a display of shamelessness that was dissected and discussed on social media, who will now judge the judge, since some netizens are practically towing the same path? The spit between the two former military heads of state began when Babangida in an interview to commemorate his 70th birthday, referred to the eight years of Obasanjo's civilian administration as a failure. Obasanjo replied by calling Babangida a "fool" to which Babangida retorted by saying that Obasanjo was a "bigger fool".

Not all Nigerians who have served, or are serving, in the public sector are sell-outs. Dr Oby Ezekwesili and Prof. Pat Utomi have successfully navigated both the public and private sector with their integrity still intact. Can any of us be more patriotic than these people? Can we be more patriotic than those who have, or had, invested their entire lives as the living conscience of those in power, like late Gani Fawehinmi and Fela Anikulapo-Kuti? These few examples are not revered today for their love for Nigeria, only on the basis of what they said or claimed to believe in, but on their unblemished records.

I point out these facts because I understand the frustration that abounds in our land. The ineptitude of the political class and establishment lackeys are legendary. This has been one of the goals of the social media—to keep the so-called "representatives" of the people in check. However, it would be hypocritical to pretend that the "People's Parliament" is without fault. The tendency to focus on people rather than on issues is gradually becoming the norm.

In any society, people differ, and express their difference though their opinions. This variety of opinions is healthy and should be encouraged. Each person has the freedom to decide which part of history to pitch his or her tent with. What matters in the end is that history also has a way of sifting out the fake from the genuine. Nonetheless, no one has a monopoly of knowledge. Ego fights and messiah complex is the fastest way to destroy the Nigeria of our dreams. It's high time to stop this senseless denigration of *I better pass my neighbour!*

Feathers Project
11 August 2012

THE NIGERIAN ONLINE ACTIVIST AND THE DANGER OF IMMEDIACY

The Nigerian blogosphere is increasingly becoming a political springboard for what I term blogotivism (blogosphere-activism). With the democratisation of the media space, an ever-increasing number of blogotivists command large constituencies of followers and now see themselves as powerful people whose voices must not only be heard, but also feared. Having drunk from the bowl of power, some have morphed into agenda setters, news framers, experts on all matters, and final social arbiters whose views, judgements and solutions must always prevail. And such solutions are not in short supply but are sadly either time bound, simplistic and/or betray an obsession with the here and now. Therein lies the danger of immediacy—that of thinking that the change we all hope for will come like a flash of lightning, or even worse, with the same immediacy of the social media. It is not as simple as think, touch, post and problem solved!

Are they in touch with the realities of the average Nigerian? This is worth asking, since many blogotivists presume to speak for most Nigerians. However, the fact remains that in this country, digital natives are still an exclusively elitist public; compared to the majority of other publics who lack internet access. It is pertinent that the Nigerian blogotivist should continually do a reality check by walking more on the streets and interacting with "everyday" people. This would yield a rich and humbling perspective that cannot be achieved via virtual communication alone. Unless we do such a reality check, most of us run the risk of developing a Messiah Complex that deifies ignorance and naivety because most of the so-called problems we scream ourselves hoarse about are not really the concern of those on the street.

While it is easy to parrot about the power of the Nigerian youth, as many blogotivists have crowned themselves emperors and empresses of the youths, it might be pertinent to ask if this also includes the majority who are in the countryside. It is simplistic to limit the definition of "youths" to those in the city, who may lack uninterrupted power but are nonetheless literate and tech-savvy. What about those who cannot go to school and rely on subsistence farming or fishing? Or the numerous almajiris who roam the streets of Sokoto? The run-of-the-mill Onitsha or Aba youth see no reason for a formal education while millions spill out of Main Market. What about the average lady in Bere, who from childhood, is confined to her mother's roadside buka selling hot amala, gbegiri and ewedu? These are the people blogotivists must find and connect with, if they are to be spared the pains of irrelevance and self-promotional posturing.

The blogotivist sees himself or herself as a member

of an elect group with a mission to clean up the mess of Nigeria and right all the wrongs of the past in one fell swoop. But can one really address rot without a proper understanding of its origins and evolution? Let us take a step back: when did this rot begin? The 1980s and 1990s saw the worst of the death knell that assigned us to an inevitable position of a failed state. The institutions that had once guaranteed our survival as a nation were violated and destroyed. The military gagged, kicked and sent to the gulag anyone who dared oppose them. Our wealth generating industries of the economy were decimated. Many Nigerians fled into exile while some of those that remained fought regardless of being in the minority. Sadly, others became passive, were bribed and/or assigned juicy posts that kept their mouths stuffed and shut perpetually. At least a man that is chewing cannot be talking at the same time. Until we do a proper assessment of the real damage caused in those years, let no one expect a sudden alleluia chorus. Structural Adjustment Programme (SAP), for instance, was one of the worst maladies inflicted upon us. Have we assessed its impact up till date? And not a wish-wash exercise but an objective peering into the ills of yesteryears. Until we have the courage to look back at the past with the fortitude of identifying our pitfalls, we may never arrive at the paradise we all desire.

When the Nazis invaded Poland, they decimated the universities, arts, music, and more. The target was to erase the Polish identity and keep Poles submissive.

The Polish Resistance was a counterforce that worked towards the preservation of their identity. The core of the movement was intellectually driven and backed with realistic but realisable goals. That resistance movement also allowed space for dialogue and conversation among its members. Take a look at blogotivists in Nigeria and tell me: Are we really having a conversation? Are we really having conversations that can rewrite the historical wrong of this nation? I do not think so. We have lots of noise and sentimental effusions of irrationality. The goal of a conversation, not argument, is understanding. And for understanding to take place, all parties involved must take turns speaking, each listening. This takes openness to the truth and a great deal of maturity to hear out those who have dissenting views. Therein lies the essence of any conversation. Unfortunately, the Nigerian blogosphere, especially some of her Twitterati, is immersed in the dictatorship of arrogance and self-deification. Most tweeps suspend their grey matter on their tablets in a hurry to prove a point. And when they meet a wall of opposition, they either hurl ad hominem slurs on their opponents or go on a victim chant.

Sadly enough, we do not realise that we are dancing to the tunes of those who wish to keep us in eternal servitude. So long as there is no conversation, there will be no change. Meanwhile, the ruining of the public still continues. What this nation needs most is a crop of intellectual minds asking the right questions backed by facts, and not those who glory in personalising insults based on hearsay. We all cannot agree, in fact, we should not agree—that is the core of a conversation. We should, however, have the ability to accept views that are totally different from ours.

The changes we seek are deep and fundamental. They will not happen immediately. Our minds must become attuned to accepting a gradualist approach to change, and more importantly to accepting that a plea for gradualism is not a sellout. As Tayo Fagbule continually insists, we must prepare our minds to accept that the change we crave may not be achieved in our lifetime. That does not mean we should fold our arms and do nothing. Rather, each should face the domain where they are competent and strive for change there. We must also realise that building requires years of industry, and that change does not happen with the snap and swiftness of our tweets and comments on blog posts. When we do this, the blogosphere then becomes best suited to aid our toil as a means to an end and not a model for instant social change. Such change belongs to the world of superman, and superman exists only in Disney world.

Feathers Project
8 January 2013

THE NIGERIAN BLOGOSPHERE: A CHANGE VESSEL OR AN ECHO CHAMBER?

The internet is a neutral tool, but its users are not. They are either fair and balanced or biased, and the Nigerian blogosphere is no exception to this rule. Consequently, there exists, in some cases, a Janus-like existence between online and traditional media.

It takes neither rocket science nor a diviner's globe to know that the netizen is, first and foremost, human. As such, the identity, bias, or even both, that a netizen expresses on issues in the blogosphere was formed *a-priori* offline. This does not mean that new habits cannot be acquired online; nonetheless, the greater part of our digital footprints are forged, not online, but in reality.

In simple terms, it may have been easier to investigate this parallelism between traditional and digital media. But the truth is that it is not that simple. The digital media provides no clear demarcation between the creator and consumer; all are lumped into an amorphous whole and are situated in one person, while for traditional media, the user is distinct from the source of the information.

Media scholars have continued to peer into the divergence and/or convergence of the new and digital media. In political communication particularly, the study of social movements and the asymmetrical relationship with old media is a case in point. The emergence of digital media initially offered "redemption" for the fecundity of the message of social movements, however, this was short-lived. Movements now face an entirely new challenge which Veronica Barassi[42] described as the "voice of one" vs. the "voice of all". This means that the blogosphere, while preserving the message of social movements without distortion (as was the case with the traditional media), also possesses the demerit of destroying the collective group identity.

In the Nigerian context, recent events provide examples for a casual examination of the blogosphere and its netizens. For instance, the BMW malfeasance of the Minister of Aviation, Stella Oduah, was a positive for investigative journalism as carried out by an online news medium because it may have ordinarily not been carried by Nigeria's traditional media. It was alleged that not only did the Ministry of Aviation purchase two armoured BMW 760 Li cars for the private use of the former minister; the agency also inflated the cost of the car over the selling price.

The Nigerian *Season of Letters* also saw the rising influence of social media as an alternative source of news. That the letter of Chief Obasanjo to President Jonathan was leaked to an online news portal illustrates two major assumptions. First, the new media has gained popular validity. Second, online news eliminates gatekeepers that monitor traditional media.

Nonetheless, the fact that the conversations of netizens have moved from traditional to digital media does not automatically translate into the veracity or credibility of news peddled. It is sad that the same online medium that broke the news of the BMW acquisition, also created a phantom Oduah MBA scandal. This media based their "investigations" on Wikipedia, which is editable by anyone, to claim that the minister has an MBA from St. Paul's College while Stella Oduah's CV as submitted to the Senate, never mentioned having such degree.

These two examples provide a representation of the dynamics of digital-traditional media relationship. Thus, a critical lens is needed for a nuanced understanding of the Nigerian blogosphere. It is also important in discovering inconsistencies in the actions and reactions of her netizens. The Nigerian blogosphere is neither an avenue for idealistic youths who are desirous for change nor is it brimming with idle "children of anger". The reality is that there are good, bad and ugly netizens. On Nigeria's Twittvilla, for instance, this perception is necessary to unpack tweets from some "overlords".

Does being online favour investigative journalism or activism? There is no direct answer to this question. The inability of traditional journalists to do their job might have led to the seeming media dependency on online media for "credible" news. However, news from the blogosphere might not always be credible. The same factors that afflict print media, in terms of ownership, also affects online media. The bias of the sponsors is hardly suppressed and might not necessarily be a clear-cut positive or negative push for investigative journalism. The demographics of tech savvy youths vs. old guards have led to an unnecessary bifurcation of good vs. evil. Just as tech-utopianism against tech-cynicism has beclouded the creativity and innovation imperative in media evaluation. The digital media has democratised information; it has delineated the space between the governed and their government. However, the extent to which it will hold leaders accountable depends on how online activism is able to substantially threaten the comfort of those in power. The righteous anger of netizens alone will not change anything. Rather, it deepens the illusion of "change" in an echo chamber.

I still wonder: Are netizens change vassals? Are they free from the malaise they point out in their leaders? Are they capable of transforming their ideals into actions? Will they move from the comfort and security of their keypads to confront the vicious terrain of political life in Nigeria?

I am afraid not.

Feathers Project
17 January 2013

BRING BACK THE BOOK: PEERS
OF AN EXPIRED EMPIRE

In Nigeria, you capture the essence of your being by the number of titles you acquire. You also must never forget the offices that you have held. Whenever you are introduced at any event, you must be introduced thus: "Former special assistant, former choir master," and an endless list of formers. Each office is like a feather on the cap of the introduced, it adds to their clout. And when former Nigerian officers go into a fight, they enter it, complete with their former offices. That was the state of things as two former public servants of the Federal Republic of Nigeria engaged in a *roforofo* fight just because of an ordinary book.

These two super intelligent warriors of a stale empire have taken to the streets and their disciples have since joined the fight. *Wahala* started with an autobiographical fiction that the twitter king's pen wrote. In his accidental hagiography, he revealed the backsides of his former peers. And not only that, his book attacked the retired emperor, the former deputy emperor and all those who were in the inner kitchen. The only one innocent amongst them was the author.

The master consolidator could not bear it. Being as canny as the twitter king, he wrote a powerful essay in which he accused the accidental author of being an intellectual fraud. Some parts of the consolidator's article read like a self-incensing compressed CV, but that is a story for another day. However, the consolidator hit the tweet king by questioning the source of his copious quotations. He wondered if the accidental author had a tape recorder or employed a ghost stenographer during the conversations he quoted in his book.

The certified ruffler of feathers, that is, the author, responded that his quotations came from journals and diaries he kept while in office. Obviously from the day he was appointed, he knew he will one day write a book and thus religiously wrote down all his conversations. And since he has a first-class degree, who dares challenge his photographic memory? Never mind that his editors made a mess of the book by inserting factual errors in the narrative. These dumb editors *sef!*

The master consolidator, who also has a first-class degree, has promised to also write his own book. There, we hope to get the full picture of his epic consolidation solution that spared Nigeria the agony of the global financial meltdown. In that book, which I anticipate will be similar to that of his colleague, the tweet king, will reveal the magic of how banking in Nigeria sailed off to the cliff, hitting the benchmark of impressive paper-only consolidation. Do not believe what that Prince of Kano did, it was only a vendetta in rehearsal and *beef,* since his intellect can never match that of our itinerant professor.

By the way, I write and make books for a living... So just in case any other member of the expired, reigning or future empires decides to tell his or her story, I hereby volunteer my services. I offer very flexible editing that indemnifies political authors from factual errors that fly into their manuscript after publication. Do not worry, it will be part of the publishing agreement and will be duly covered by a reasonable fee. That will be my "little" contribution to bringing back the book! *Ndi ala!*

Feathers Project
10 May 2013

NARRATIVES OF NIGERIA'S
POLITICO-TWITTERATI

The streets of Twitter Nigeria are hot and harsh these days. The clash of the politico-twitterati on each side of the divide has been characterised by vile tweet-blood. Politico-Twitterati are those influential overlords who are active partisan politicians. They differ from "political tweeps", or political activists who, though they tweet on politics, owe no allegiance to any political party.

The narrative as expounded by each side of the divide can be grouped into two: disruptive narration by the opposition and confutative narration by the establishment.

The Disruptive Narrative of the Opposition Politico-Twitterati

A casual observation of the handles of some opposition overlords reveals that they thrive on rumours. It seems as though they patiently wait for any gaffe from government officials and then precipitate a tweet storm. For instance, take the "news" of the fifty-three gold-plated iPhones that were ordered for Nigeria's independence celebrations, or that of the president dropping the title of "Commander-in-Chief" for non-military functions. In both cases, the opposition overlords ranted and cursed. Sadly, they neither substantiated the rumours (for the fifty-three gold-plated iPhones) nor read beyond the headlines.

When the rumours are well founded, like the reprehensible acquisition of two armoured BMW cars for the Minister of Aviation's personal use, by a cash strapped aviation agency, their focus was usually from an "all or none" angle. Rather than decry the scandalous act and propose an action plan, our opposition overlords go over the top with rage. However, this anger is basically narcissist and mired by denigrating tweets. Any tweep that dares think outside their defined boundaries is either a "closet" PDP voltron or a "confirmed" government apologist. I will save my ink for an awkward attempt at defending the purchase of armoured BMW cars for the aviation minister.

Generally, the Nigerian opposition politico-twitterati are afflicted with the same malaise as the Nigerian opposition parties. Their exclusive mantra seems to be to get the PDP out of government, and this has coloured their narrative. Their lack of originality and delusion that freedom of speech equals freedom to spite is nauseating. Unfortunately, their "courage" to dispense copious bile is not, and must not be, mistaken for either true courage or patriotism. It is also not a virtue, and to persist in seeing it as a virtue is self-deceit.

The Confutative Narrative of the Establishment Politico-Twitterati

The establishment overlords suffer a malignant refutation narrative. Many of them are only on Twitter to debunk actions, imagined and real, of the opposition. Or how else can one explain that the official establishment tweep, the adviser on #twitterthings, spends his time tweeting parables. And when he is not preaching, he perpetually engages the numero uno accidental public servant in a tweet-fight. Even though our president is active on Facebook, it is inexcusable that his twitter handle @JGoodluckTweets has been dormant since May 2011.

The establishment media team on Twitter is a complete disaster. For instance, in the alleged iPhones ruse, there was no factual rebuttal from the establishment overlords. What we got were sentimental tweets that blamed the opposition. It took an independent political tweep to investigate and refute the allegation. Same goes for quoting the aviation minister out of context. It also took a neutral party to get these facts on table.

Another sad case is the un-bulking and privatisation of the Power Holding Company of Nigeria. An event of such magnitude, in which the government handed over electricity distribution to fourteen private companies, was no news on Twitter. Perhaps some of the establishment overlords were taking a siesta, except for two fellows. And as is the norm, many tweeps got wind of this landmark event via a non-partisan tweep who could not stand the unjustified silence.

The principal aim of marketing is not to disprove your rival but to sell the merits of your product. Rumours thrive in the absence of factual information. Besides, effective public relation is a deliberate, planned and sustained effort to create goodwill with the public. It is about time the government tweeps wake up, do their jobs and stop blaming the opposition. It is time they moved away from reactively responding to proactive engagement.

Feathers Project
20 October 2013

WHY I AM A "FENCIST"

Twitter Nigeria has been boiling for some months now. As the general elections in February approach, campaigns are nearing a crescendo. Currently, there is a vicious division between supporters of the ruling Peoples' Democratic Party (PDP) and the opposition All Progressives Congress (APC). The lies, blackmails, accusations and counter accusations between both sides have assumed epic proportions. In view of the above, I have decided to sit firmly on the fence.

The shouting match on whose presidential candidate is better than the other is all one hears on Twitter these days. Unfortunately, this "my-candidate-better-pass-your-candidate" debate has spiralled into mudslinging that makes motor park touts look good. Rarely are issues discussed. When they come up, the argumentum ad hominem path is taken. More often than not, one notices so many "logical fallacies". Some folks seem to have patented the franchise of making unsubstantiated opinions which they present as equivocal "facts".

I do not begrudge those who have taken sides, or those who have firmly dug into their respective trenches as supporters of either President Goodluck Ebele

Jonathan (GEJ) or General Muhammadu Buhari (GMB). As a matter of fact, I respect them, for it is no mean feat to consistently stand behind a candidate on the streets of TwitterNG. It matters nothing if these e-supporters are hired for their services or if they do so purely out of "patriotic" zeal. It is their choice and I respect their freedom of association.

Nonetheless, I will not be persuaded into joining the fray, a simplistic reduction of the presidential candidates, or their parties as the "messiah". Nigeria is too large and complicated to be reduced to one man or woman having the key to reset all our woes. As a matter of fact, no single person, living or dead, holds the exclusive prescription to our national malaise. This is why I hope that the fanatic supporters of both candidates will be civil enough to respect my decision to remain on the fence. It is my choice and I don't see why it is so difficult to accept "Fencism" as a legitimate position.

Some folks have already ascribed divine omnipotence to themselves: that ability to read minds and to question the free decision of others. For some, a "fencist" is a traitor that sits idle while Nigeria burns. The only "legitimate" freedom, according to them, consists in taking a stand, for or against. You cannot sit on the fence; you are either on one of its sides. It must either be for or against GEJ or GMB. *Odiegwu!* It does not stop there; you MUST profess the credo of your support all day long on Twitter.

However, I am yet to see how their vicious rants and tweet fights translate into patriotism.

Fencism is not neutralism! I have my political bias, but I will not be bullied into displaying it on Twitter. Fencism is objectivity, realising that both candidates have their flaws and not turning a blind eye, as many do, to them. Fencism is having the courage to tweet for and against any of the candidates. It is about not being held bound by the fanatical slavery of "my-candidate-better-pass your-candidate". Fencism also does not mean that I am apolitical, as I will exercise my voting rights on Election Day. I have only refused to waste my precious time only tweeting about the elections.

In my "yard", the fence is sturdy and impermeable. The space on the fence also has an infinite coefficient of expansion. You are free not to accept my Fencism; no big deal but at least, respect it.

Feathers Project
12 January 2014

VIRTUES 4.0 FOR WEB 2.0?

With the 2015 general elections drawing close, the Nigerian tweetsphere have become dangerously polarised. The dominance of two major political parties—the Peoples' Democratic Party and the All Progressives Congress—also means that the "narratives of Nigeria's politico-twitterati" are more disruptive than ever. As though that were not enough, the propensity with which tweeps transform rumours and outright lies into exclusive "news" is alarming. This might be a good time to suggest some tips for those who value their credibility and wish to preserve it.

The English word *cardinal* comes from the Latin word *cardo*, which means "hinge." All other virtues hinge on these four: prudence, justice, fortitude, and temperance. Plato first discussed the cardinal virtues in the *Republic*, and they found their way into Christian teachings through Plato's disciple, Aristotle. Let us take these virtues one after the other.

Prudence has been classified as the first cardinal virtue, because it is concerned with intellect. Aristotle defined prudence as *recta ratio agibilium*, meaning "right reason applied to practice." In other words, prudence is practical wisdom. When we mistake evil for good, we are not exercising prudence; in fact, we are showing our lack of it. It is only through prudence that we can seek the counsel of others, due to our propensity for making mistakes. It is imprudent to assume that we know it all and this seems to be the natural lure of many twitterati! In this current volatile clime, tweeps should realise that it is imprudent to jump into every conversation or to make generalising assertions that are simply indefensible. A prudent person should avoid embarrassing situations of bravado. A prudent person is not a "clever tactician" who repeatedly escapes personal commitment. Prudence is not "timidity" but being afraid to make a decision or making it known when justice demands it.

Justice is the second cardinal virtue, because it is concerned with will-power. Justice simply means giving each person their due. Justice is not revenge, but the conservation of rights. Consequently, justice in its proper sense is positive. Injustice occurs when individuals or the society deprive others that which they are owed.

There is a growing tendency to assume that since the talking space is free of gatekeepers, therefore one is also "free" to malign or destroy the "good" or "bad" names of others. However, it is very important to refrain from the herd mentality when issues occur and consider if there are other angles to a story, as they are wont to on Twitter. This is especially important if we do not possess all the facts to a story. It will no longer matter if the court of public opinion has already given a verdict. But what if their judgement is false?

Fortitude is commonly called courage. However, this is different from the conceptualisation we have of courage today; particularly the Twitter type. Real fortitude helps us to overcome fear and remain steadfast in the face of adversities. However, since fortitude relates to will-power, it is always rational. Therefore, fortitude does not admit danger for the sake of *gragra* or *shakara*. Fortitude is neither foolishness nor rashness. Please think before you tweet. If you want to exercise your courage, try the streets!

Temperance is the restraint of our desires or passions. Temperance moderates excesses, and as such, requires the balancing of legitimate goods against our inordinate desire for them. Our legitimate use of such goods may be different at different times; temperance is the "golden mean".

Itchy fingers are often associated with being the first to know and that inordinate passion to claim bragging rights of being the first to tweet. Before you tweet, take a chill pill, breathe in and chill again: there is no award for being the first to tweet. It is true that your grandmother has always praised your intelligence, yet smartness is knowing when to "jump pass". Pride is exercising no restraint on the desires of our thought through speech or via our writing.

African Hadithi
12 March 2014

INNOCENT OR VIRULENT NETIZENS?

The conversation among scholars and enthusiasts has morphed from *if* social media has changed the landscape to *how* this change is being perpetuated. While the crushing of gatekeepers, the inherent freedom and participatory nature of social media platforms, is no longer novel, the effects of the crush continue affecting various aspects of life. Nigeria currently occupies an enviable position on the blogosphere of the continent, with Nigerians ranked as one of the top three tweeters in Africa.

Numerous discussions on this rising profile of the once hidden voices seem to be limited on this new-found power. This also includes, but is not limited to, the merits of technology granting unfettered access to the average person on the street, and the impressive impact that being wired up has created. The ability to make government accountable to the governed and giving an instant right of reply to netizens is celebrated across board.

Of course, this is no mean feat. Governments, especially in Nigeria, have a history of glorifying the absurd. A case in point is the sudden disappearance, and equally mysterious re-appearance of a Nigerian Twitter user, Ciaxon, who shared sensitive security pictures via his handle recently. The prudence or imprudence of tweeting and sharing pictures during such a delicate operation is however, a story for another day.

It is important to ask: who keeps watch over these online watchers? How do we guarantee that this freedom of expression, of a free and open internet, is not abused? What happens when netizens jump from protectors of freedom to guardians of a new gaol?

A few days ago, the Nigerian twitterati focused their attention and energy on the deputy minister of defence. Guess what the minister's "unpardonable crime" was? He tweeted, drinking beer on Easter Sunday! He later deleted it and stated that his account was hacked. Despite this, the self-anointed tweet overlords were not pacified; they ranted nonstop.

It might be trite to recall that freedom is not absolute. The bastion of Western democracy is still calling for the head of Edward Snowden. As much as we celebrate the power of social media and will do everything to ensure it remains free from government emasculation, nonetheless is it so difficult for netizens to exercise a corresponding responsibility? It takes little effort to be an amplifier of news. All that is required is to retweet and think later. What is more necessary, and more tasking, is to validate news on social media. Yet, even news validators need a tinge of healthy scepticism, independence and rationality.

The follow-follow mania in the Nigeria twittersphere can be quite depressing.

Are netizens innocent or virulent *per se?* I will say no. However, netizens bear the personal responsibility to either keep their innocence or inflict virulence on social media platforms. The choice is ours.

Feathers Project
22 April 2014

REFRAMING NIGERIA'S TERROR NARRATIVE

Boko Haram (BH) recently claimed responsibility for another terrorist violation of the Nigerian people. However, this time around, BH's leader, Abubakar Shekau was incensed that they were not given due credit for the explosions in Lagos: "A bomb went off in Lagos. I ordered the bomber who went and detonated it, you said it was a fire incident, well if you hide it from people, you can't hide it from Allah."[43]

With such a display of arrogance, do we need any more proof that BH loves being in the media spotlight? The fact that the Lagos explosions were either hidden from public gaze or were better managed in the media, hit a raw nerve in Shekau's media thirsty ego. Unlike the Movement for the Emancipation of the Niger Delta (MEND) which had an "apparently" efficient media presence via their constant media alerts of impending bombings via emails, BH seems to feast on indirect publicity. There lies the irony that Nigerian citizens—victims of BH's attack—are the mouthpiece of the terrorists. Clearly, BH's "haram" does not extend to publicity. On the contrary, their proficient use of YouTube and their dispersion through a certain foreign channel suggests a clear western media "halal" and indeed, a growing obsession with such publicity.

Soon after Shekau's admittance of being behind the Abuja and Lagos bomb blasts, I had an interesting conversation on Twitter. It started with this tweet by @feathersproject: "Obviously, Shekau is furious that he and BH were not 'credited' by the media for another bomb pop. It means he loves the attention."

I advocated a media blackout on BH terror and this naturally ignited a heated discussion. Obviously, the thrust of my suggestions of snuffing out BH's relish of deaths from the news was not generally accepted. It had generated similar sentiments some years earlier during a Public Relations seminar. I, and some others, had advocated the following:

"100 Percent Media Blackout on all Boko Haram Activities: As it stands, Boko Haram has won the psychological warfare by instilling fear amongst Nigerians. Boko Haram has used the media to issue threats, spread the details of their successful activities and to promise more attacks. We therefore suggest a radical change in this information war: a total media blackout.

"Centralised Media Mouthpiece: We propose an integrated and synchronised communication strategy for BH. As such, all media briefings, press conferences, interviews, press releases, reactions, etc.... must receive the implicit endorsement of the head of the media team

on Boko Haram. The head of this team will also be the exclusive spokesman on Boko Haram issues in Nigeria. However, there will be an alternate head— who he/she can delegate this duty to—only when the head is not available or is indisposed."[44]

Many disagreed with these approaches and I must admit that those who opposed the blanket media silence had strong points. Their fear, which was quite reasonable, was that the government would definitely go to sleep. These were not unfounded considering the apparent institutional decay and the cynicism with government's "truths". Also, it was argued that it would be a grave injustice to the victims and their families if their plights were to go unnoticed. This additional wound of lack of public empathy would be too much for people already devastated, the argument continued. Faced with such valid objections, I had to change my original propositions to @feathersproject's question on "how do we make sure government protects and destroys terror without gagging the voice of the voiceless victims?"

I do not claim to have all the answers. Besides I am not deluded to think that Nigeria's war on terror will be won via media strategies alone. Nonetheless, literature on media and social movements confirm the importance of news framing. Frank Luntz's apt statement which captures the essence of framing goes thus: "It's not what you say; it's how you say it."[45] It is significant to dwell on news framing because the audience depends on media, not only for information, but also to make decisions. As such, the media provides "a window" for the audience to "understand" an issue.

How then do we reframe the single terror story without falling into the trap of propaganda or gagging the victims of BH's terror? Do we have the courage to side step our entrenched political convictions to face the common enemy, BH? Or is this an impossible task, laced with the inherent danger of gagging free speech? I admit that a total blackout is untenable based on the prevailing circumstances. However, a reframing of the terror narrative is long overdue.

African Hadithi
17 July 2014

BEYOND AN #EBOLAFREENIGERIA

The World Health Organisation (WHO) on Monday, 20 October 2014 certified Nigeria free of the Ebola Virus Disease (EVD). A statement from the organisation headlined "Nigeria is Now Free of the Ebola Virus Transmission" reads:

> The lines on the tabular situation reports, sent to WHO each day by its country office in Nigeria, have now been full of zeros for 42 days. WHO officially declares that Nigeria is now free of Ebola virus transmission.

> This is a spectacular success story that shows that Ebola can be contained. The story of how Nigeria ended what many believed to be potentially the most explosive Ebola outbreak imaginable is worth telling in detail. Such a story can help the many other developing countries that are deeply worried by the prospect of an imported Ebola case and eager to improve their preparedness plans. Many wealthy countries, with outstanding health systems, may have something to learn as well.[46]

Ebola's ravaging of West African countries like Liberia and Sierra Leone, and its recent outbreak in Texas, has generated global panic. Some infected healthcare workers who were administered a vaccine that is yet to undergo full clinical trial have recovered. The unavailability, however, of any true and tried treatment or vaccine has made the Ebola epidemic a cause of anxiety. In light of these facts, Nigeria's successful curtailment of the disease is cause for hope and excitement, not only for Nigeria, but for other countries as well.

Patrick Sawyer, an American-Liberian lawyer infected with the virus, died in Lagos, Nigeria's commercial city. Upon arrival from Liberia, where he had taken care of a sick Ebola relative, Mr Sawyer collapsed at the airport. He was rushed to a hospital, where he was initially treated for malaria. He died days later. Mr Sawyer was diagnosed of Ebola some days before his death.[47]

A World-Class Epidemiological Detective Work

Dr Ameyo Adadevoh, the consultant who treated Sawyer, was instrumental in preventing Ebola from becoming an epidemic in Nigeria. Dr Adadevoh placed Mr Sawyer in quarantine and refused to discharge him despite pressure from high quarters. She was reported to have contracted Ebola on 4 August 2014 and died from the disease on 19 August 2014.

Lagos is Africa's most populous city, and for a disease outbreak of this dimension, it was a keg of gun powder waiting to explode. The explosion, however, never occurred. According to *Scientific America*, Nigeria's success was based on the following:

- *Fast and thorough tracing of all potential contacts*
- *Ongoing monitoring of all of these contacts*
- *Rapid isolation of potentially infectious contacts.*
  The swift battle was won, not only with vigilant
  disinfecting, port-of-entry screening and rapid
  isolation, but also with boot leather and a lot of in-
  person follow-up visits, numbering about 18,500
  who undertook the search for possible new cases
  of Ebola among a total of 989 identified contacts.
  Such ground-level work may sound extreme.
  Even the oft meticulous WHO declared the feat
  "a piece of world-class epidemiological detective
  work."[48]

Nigeria's effective public health response, hinged on an existing Incident Management Centre established for poliomyelitis, was deployed for managing Ebola. According to the Centre for Disease Control:

> *Directly linked to contact tracing was the Social*
> *Mobilisation Strategy. This included teams of three*
> *social mobilisers who were trained and deployed*
> *to conduct house-to-house, in-person visits within*
> *specific radii of the homes of Ebola contacts. For high-*
> *density areas, house-to-house teams covered a 500m*
> *radius, 1km in medium density areas and 2km for low*
> *density. As of 24 September, approximately 26,000*
> *households of persons living around Ebola contacts had*
> *been reached with house-to-house visits in Lagos and*
> *Rivers states.[49]*

Besides the epidemiological response, some Nigerian professionals used social media for information dissemination. One such initiative was the Ebola Alert, "an evidence-driven group of volunteer professionals working on Ebola Virus Disease Interventions." They used a Twitter feed to keep people informed and to dispel rumours, as rumour-mongering could be devastating in such crisis situations.

The Lagos state government plans to send health professionals to Sierra Leone to aid in the containment of the Ebola Virus Disease ravaging the country. Nonetheless, Nigeria should not rest on this current certification from WHO of being Ebola free. Nor should we get caught up in petty squabbles such as the one between the Federal Ministry of Health and the Lagos state government over who deserves credit for Nigeria's containment of the disease.

The price of freedom is eternal vigilance. Ebola is not dead until it is eradicated from all parts of the globe and can no longer pose a threat to humanity.

Global Voices
27 August 2014

Postscript

#EbolaFreeNigeria was significant because of the utilisation of social media, especially Twitter for social good. During the Ebola epidemic the Nigerian public was really traumatised because of government's history of ineptitude. Also considering that the disease was fatal and with no cure added to the panic that reached paranoid heights during those times. It was therefore a great good that was done by the #EbolaAlert that utilised Twitter to dispel unfounded rumours during the epidemic. One of such instances was a message that went viral via social media that the best prevention to contacting Ebola was through salt water bath and also drinking the salt water first thing in the morning. The effect of this rumour was devastating since salt aggravates the health of hypertensive patients.

In addition, #EbolaFreeNigeria was a counter balance to the news imbalance that the continent experienced during that Ebola pandemic. Western media framed the pandemic to whip up the frenzy of their citizens who became obsessed about a possible Ebola "invasion" of their respective countries. The net effect was that rather than raise awareness about the disease, force governments and multi-national pharmaceutical companies to withdraw their patent to the vaccine, the Western framing only aggravated panic and subtle racism. The same was played out in the succeeding article, which suggests that all lives are not really equal because the African life is more dispensable.

However, it is unfortunate that the heroes/heroines of that paid the supreme sacrifice with their lives for the #EbolaFreeNigeria are yet to be honoured by the

Nigerian government. Chief among which is Dr Ameyo Adadevoh who stood her ground and prevented the index case patient from leaving the hospital. This tells a lot about the insolence of the Nigerian government but a lot more about the heroism of the ordinary Nigerian. Dr Ameyo Adadevoh is the real heroine of contemporary Nigeria and she deserves a posthumous national award for losing her life to save lives.

BAGA MASSACRE VS. CHARLIE HEBDO ATTACK: SIMILAR STORIES, DIFFERENT NARRATIVES

Baga, a town in the north-eastern state of Borno, Nigeria, suffered unimaginable catastrophe recently when Boko Haram, Nigeria's vampires of death, slaughtered its innocent residents. Amnesty International described it as the Islamist militant group's "deadliest massacre in recent history."[50] Controversy rages between the official estimates of a hundred and fifty deaths against the two thousand reported by other independent sources.

However, this horrid news did not make global headlines as much as the Paris attacks[51] that left seventeen people dead. While many reasons abound for the media silence, in this case it appears to be a combination of three factors: the nearness news factor, the numbing callousness of Nigeria's political elites—both the ruling party and the opposition—and a compromised local press.

#IamCharlie, but #IamBaga too!

Baga is an out-of-the-way town tucked in the impermeable Borno state. Most places within north-eastern Nigeria, bordering Chad, Niger and Cameroon, are now controlled by Boko Haram. Nigeria's former chief of defence staff,

Air Chief Marshal Alex Badeh, stated that Boko Haram had seized the headquarters of a multinational military force located on Nigeria's border after Chad and Niger had withdrawn its forces from the base.

This means that neither journalists nor bloggers have full access to Baga and cannot give the exact assessment of the situation on ground. This is a direct opposite of the horror that gripped Paris, an easily accessible city full of netizens wielding smartphones. In an article for *The Conversation,* Global Voices co-founder Ethan Zukerman expounded:

> *Paris is a highly connected global city with thousands of working journalists, while Baga is isolated, difficult and dangerous to reach. The attacks on Charlie Hebdo targeted journalists, and it's understandable that journalists would cover the death of their comrades. The attacks in Paris were a shock and a surprise, while deaths at the hands of Boko Haram have become distressingly common in an insurgency that has claimed over ten thousand lives since 2009.[52]*

Nonetheless this does not totally extricate the complicity of Western mainstream media. Correspondent Simon Allison wrote in a piece for a South African news site *Daily Maverick,* that "African lives are still deemed less newsworthy—and, by implication, less valuable—than western lives."[53]

Some Nigerians are of the view that the country deserves more assistance from the global community against Boko Haram's unending murders. For instance, Ignatius Kaigama, the Catholic Archbishop of Jos, Nigeria, thinks that the global solidarity accorded the Paris violence should also be shown to Nigerians. "We need that spirit to be spread around. Not just when it (an attack) happens in Europe, but when it happens in Nigeria, in Niger, in Cameroon," he told the BBC.[54]

"The Outrage is almost Non-Existent"

As much as the global media conspiracy of silence seems inviting, it neither does justice to the complex nature of the Baga massacre nor exonerates Nigeria's callous political leadership. Less than twenty-four hours after the Charlie Hebdo massacre in Paris, Nigerian President Goodluck Jonathan issued a statement[55] condemning that "dastardly terrorist attack" but kept mute on similar but more devastating attacks at home.

However, about a week after the Baga incident, the president visited Borno state. A statement by his spokesman stated that President Jonathan told "officers and soldiers of the Division that the nation was very proud of them and grateful for their dedication and commitment to the defence of the civilian population against terrorists and violent extremists."[56] Nonetheless, this criticism is not reserved for the government alone, but also extends to opposition politicians trying to score cheap political points from the Baga catastrophe.

It is election season in Nigeria, and as such, the local media is more concerned with advertisements from politicians, by covering their campaign train than any factual reporting. The Nigerian media is as much complicit in maintaining a silence on Baga as their foreign counterparts. The complicated mess of the Baga situation was best summed up by this Facebook post from a San Francisco based author and editor, Jeremy Adams Smith:

> *The first thing you'll notice is that there is not a lot of coverage of the massacres in Baga and Askira; in many papers, it's totally unmentioned and invisible. Why this crime is not being covered IN NIGERIA, I'll address in a moment. But what you do see in the papers is a lot of finger-pointing and rage against the government of Nigeria; of course, it's election season. It's the job of that government to protect its people, and the government is not doing its job. [...] The government of Nigeria doesn't want you to know, isn't transparent, and isn't helping people who are suffering. In fact, there is widespread denial throughout Nigeria of what is happening—a denial that extends to the press.[57]*

#IamBaga will certainly not trend as much as #JeSuiCharlie has for these reasons. Nonetheless, as much as there is glaring evidence of a global media blackout on Baga, this does not mean that the Nigerian government is free from blame. At the same time, the local press cannot be canonised. In Nigeria, human life is almost of no value, the Nigerian life is worth nothing, absolutely nothing! This is evident in the way that government reacts in the face of human disasters that result in the death of Nigerians. On the other hand, in places like Paris, the human life has worth and is treated with dignity. This is seen in the response of government to any calamity that affects her citizens. In addition, BH had had repeated blasts in the north-east. And Baga was just one of the communities. The average Nigerian— including the leadership—is used to the sound of blasts or the reports of blasts and they meet it with silence. Hence, there was nothing unique about Baga. In the end, it is a combination of all these that make the injustice of the Baga slaughter blood-curdling.

Global Voices
16 January 2015

TIME FOR HOPE AND HEALING IN NIGERIA

The Nigerian people's 28 March vote for General Muhammadu Buhari as their president-elect was unprecedented but unsurprising, given the massive campaign by Buhari's All Progressive Congress before the general elections. The concession of defeat by incumbent President Goodluck Jonathan was equally unprecedented, and it saved the country from post-election violence. Nonetheless, Nigeria voted as a deeply fragmented nation. While Buhari got a majority of his votes from most of the north and south-west, Goodluck got block votes from the south-south and south-east. In other words, neither of them got majority votes from areas outside his region.

Nigeria is a presidential democracy with thirty-six states and three tiers of government—local, state, and federal. Its diversity—over two hundred and fifty ethnic nationalities and more than five hundred languages—is a source of strength but also a weakness. The 2015 general elections have once again highlighted the country's deeply-entrenched regional politics. While the south fears northern domination, the north feels cheated out of governance.

The effects of the Nigerian Civil War (1967-70)

which include religious fundamentalism, and its resultant violence, are still pervasive. This will be the biggest test of the Buhari presidency: engineering a national reconciliation. He will have to "move back" and address the deep roots of ethnocentrism, in order to eventually move forward.

Besides national reconciliation, the incoming president will have to focus on addressing corruption. This was one of Buhari's campaign promises, which he reiterated in his acceptance speech on 1 April: "Furthermore, we shall strongly battle another form of evil that is even worse than terrorism, the evil of corruption...I repeat that corruption will not be tolerated by this administration."[58] Now, the president-elect's task is to match his words with actions, keeping in mind the high hopes that Nigerians have in him.

But corruption can only be curtailed when the present culture of impunity is no longer the order of the day. This is one area that the Jonathan government failed to address; in fact, Jonathan was surrounded by people who were, in the court of public opinion, drenched in the filth of corrupt practices.

Will Buhari do better? The president-elect is known for his zero tolerance for putridity in governance. However, his closest collaborators reek of a vitiated past. Will he be willing to persecute his close allies if they are found culpable by a competent court of having amassed wealth through illicit means? And will the president-elect extend the corruption crusade to legislators and the judiciary as well? Only time will tell and test the resolve of General Buhari.

Jonathan's major albatross was security, especially in the context of the Boko Haram insurgency in the northeast. Most Nigerians were struck by the lack of direction and apparent helplessness of their government in countering the violent insurgency. Jonathan's government did make a significant impact in the last few weeks before the elections by quelling the insurgents and recovering parts of Nigeria that were under Boko Haram's control. But these measures came too late, and by then Nigerians had decided they wanted a more forceful commander-in-chief for their armed forces.

Buhari has an impressive resume. He fought for the unity of Nigeria as a soldier and understands the inner workings of the military. This is no mean feat in a country whose Armed Forces are as polarised as the civilian population. Still, he has an uphill task ahead to reverse the perceived politicisation of the Boko Haram insurgency.

Yet, there is hope for the deeply-fragmented nation, and Buhari has received the mandate of the Nigerian people for this task. There was no post-election violence and the election itself was free and fair by global standards—all positive signs for moving forward. Buhari must now restore healing to his people.

Gateway House
9 April 2015

THE UNTOLD STORY OF SOCIAL MEDIA AND THE 2015 NIGERIAN ELECTIONS

Hope swept across the continent following the inauguration of Muhammadu Buhari as Nigeria's president on 29 May 2015. President Buhari had defeated the incumbent, Goodluck Jonathan. Not only was this unusual, but the attendant concession of defeat by Goodluck was remarkable, especially in a continent saturated by sit-tight leaders. However, there is another element, albeit still untold, to the election: the social media story.

This will not be the first time social media has played a part in Nigerian elections. The 2011 general election bears an imprint of the power of social media in Nigerian politics. Goodluck Jonathan was the first Nigerian president to join Facebook. In his book, *My Friends and I*, it was on Facebook that he declared his intention to run for president in 2011. This, according to Nigerian journalist, Tolu Ogunlesi, led to the "faddification" of Facebook in Nigerian politics:

> *President Jonathan took the shine off the IBB presidential declaration in Abuja by choosing that morning to announce his own bid on Facebook.*

Ibrahim Babangida launched a YouTube campaign video, and had an aide boast that he had become an avid Facebooker.[59]

Similarly, one of the reasons attributed to the goodwill enjoyed by Muhammadu Buhari's re-branding and eventual ascendancy to the presidency was propelled by his social media strategy. CNN journalist Lauren Said-Moorhouse reported that:

Social media has globally become one of the most important tools for candidates during election campaigns—and Nigeria's race was no exception. Cynthia Mbamalu, programs manager at Nigerian youth charity YIAGA, said platforms like Twitter and Facebook helped the Buhari campaign to reach population pockets that they could have otherwise missed. "Social media provided the opportunity to connect with Nigerians, especially young people," she explains. "For the first time in a long while, there were tweets targeted mainly at promoting the person of General Buhari and the party's vision for Nigeria."[60]

It was therefore not surprising that President Buhari, in his inaugural speech, acknowledged that "the Nigerian press is the most vibrant in Africa." His tacit gratitude to his supporters and critics on social media was also not lost on observers: "My appeal to the media today—and this includes the social media—is to exercise its considerable powers with responsibility and patriotism."[61]

Social Media Propelled the Political "War"

Twitter in Nigeria is a vibrant pool of conversation. This mirrors the Nigerian society itself, which "is such a vibrant place that even the most mundane is crackling with energy." Christian Purefoy, director of news at the entertainment channel BattaBox, asserted in 2012 that, "With the explosion of mobile phones (and their video cameras) and the coming of the internet—there are now tools in the hands of every Nigerian to explore, share and make their voices heard."[62]

Twitter became a battleground for supporters of the two main presidential candidates, Buhari and Jonathan. The atrocious "war" was divisive, as each party dug firmly in their respective trenches. Those who were indifferent watched keenly and later made up their minds. However, a different conceptualisation of political participation was conceived on Twitter Nigeria, namely "Fencism." As I explained in a piece for *The Scoop* earlier this year:

> *Fencism is not neutralism! I have my political bias, but I will not be bullied into displaying it on Twitter. Fencism is objectivism, realising that both candidates have their flaws and not turning a blind eye—as many do—on them. Fencism is having the courage to tweet for and against any of the candidates. Not being held*

under the fanatical slavery of my candidate better pass
your candidate. Fencism also means that I will vote
on that day and will not also waste my precious time
tweeting about the elections.[63]

This stance was contentious as some Twitter users
thought it was hypocritical and a cover-up for hiding
entrenched political bias. However, the war got real on the
blogosphere as the election results were being collated.
Tony Egbulefu reported:

Late in the evening on Saturday, 28 March, social
media users hit the net with the report that President
Goodluck Jonathan had lost in the two Aso Rock
polling units. The post went viral in an instant and
buoyed the hopes of the All Progressives Congress
(APC) supporters that such loss by the president
within the perimeters of the seat of power could only be
an indicator of matters that could go worse for him in
the wider, far-flung political space. It turned out that
the president won in Unit 021, which was located
nearer to the seat of power with 293 votes against
Buhari's 263, while Buhari won in Unit 022, located
in the outer reaches with 348 to 302. […]
No matter the perspectives, it is a hard fact that the
social media proved handy in bringing anxious
Nigerians up-to-speed with the voting outcomes.
From Facebook alone, many became certain of the

direction the wind would blow, well ahead of President Jonathan's Tuesday evening concession of victory to Gen. Muhammadu Buhari, and Prof. Attahiru Jega's early Wednesday morning election returns.[64]

Propaganda and Hate Speech

Besides the campaign rants and propaganda present on the Nigerian blogosphere, this election also witnessed a cross-pollination of news from social media to mainstream media. Since netizens offer more opportunities of immediacy, the Nigerian mainstream media had to play catch-up many times. However, the downside of this was that traditional media fell for unverified news that sprang from social media during the elections. It was a season of propaganda unlimited. Opeyemi Agbaje opined that:

This was one Nigerian election that was decided largely on account of propaganda and messaging! The [opposition] APC's "change" message was compelling, and the campaign stayed on this message throughout the campaign. This effective message was complemented with devastating deployment of propaganda, often false or contrived, but which most voters believed. President Jonathan's [and the People's Democratic Party] communication machinery was in response hapless! A [...] ruling party could be so completely incoherent in its communication that it was soon portrayed in the media (and sometimes in its own mindset) as a de facto

*opposition party. The election also marked the coming
of age of social media as a critical force in Nigerian
politics, for good or bad!⁶⁵*

Emmanuel Onwubiko gave a glimpse into the hate speech
prevalent in Nigeria's blogosphere during the elections:

*It is regrettable that popular social media platforms
like Facebook, Twitter, and Instagram, among others,
have become potent weapons for near diabolical attacks
targeted at political opponents as Nigeria prepares to
hold one of the most contentious general elections in over
five decades or indeed since after Nigeria gained her so-
called flag independence from the British overlords in
1960. The 2015 general elections have been turned
into a theatre of hate speeches and campaigns coloured
in a form that defies logic and common sense. Various
politically motivated hate speeches about various
candidates and especially the two leading presidential
candidates of the All Progressives Congress and the
Peoples' Democratic Party have been bandied. I am
sure if experts should collate analyses of contents of the
social media this year, Nigeria will rank tops because
arguably more than 40 million young Nigerians who
have since graduated and have no means of livelihood
have found solace in the various social media platforms
and are busy churning out divergent messages.⁶⁶*

Nonetheless, the truth is that Nigeria's social media ecosystem has undergone an amazing transformation over the years. Whether it evolves into a platform that propels or hinders change, is a story for another day. What is obvious is that henceforth, no Nigerian politician can afford to run for office without first sharpening their social media presence tools.

Global Voices
23 June 2015

#TROLLCABAL NIGERIA AND THE REINVENTION
OF INTERNET TROLLING

Social networking sites (SNS) have expanded to become both a network and a communication medium. The inherent potentials of this digital platform to expand participatory democracy have continued to draw the attention of scholars and practitioners. The reason is that for many years the decline of youth participation in politics has morphed into a lure. However, the Arab Springs of Northern African countries basically dismantled this assumption to show that digital natives are not shrinking from political participation, rather their tool and engagement has only changed.

Nonetheless, social media and indeed, online networks also have a dark side. The anonymity of users has essentially propelled the use of digital as the channel of abuses and insults. To be more specific, social media has deepened the space for forging new identities and their inherent demerits. In other words, the Internet has provided a virtual space that encourages users to forge and sustain a new identity which might be at complete variance to their offline personas. The digital media also provides these users with a platform to amplify their constructive or destructive online identities.[67] One of the reasons for this is that some people seek to "escape" from their routine offline life. This is achieved through role-playing. However, "not all role–playing is positive, just as not all role–playing is escapist. While in some cases role–playing can be a means of working through issues and insecurities experienced off–line, sometimes role–play can merely be acting out the same problems in an endless feedback loop."[68]

In view of this, one then appreciates the engagement of scholars with destructive and disruptive online personas who have been named trolls. The impact of trolls' role-playing and identity will be the focus of the next section.

Who is a Troll?

The first definition of a troll was expounded by Donath (1999) who described trolling as an identity game. The troll presents the classical literary picture of Dr Hyde and Mr Jekyll – a Janus-faced contrasting personality. Donath emphasised that "the troll attempts to pass as a legitimate participant, sharing the group's common interests and concerns."[69] However this is mere role-switching, the appearance of belonging but with the main agenda of causing disruption. Dahlberg (2001) asserts that: "…after developing their false identity and becoming accepted within a group, the troll sets about disrupting proceedings while trying to maintain his or her cover".[70] In other words, a troll is not pleasant; a troll can destroy a social-media-mediated online network and/or community.

> *A troll can disrupt the discussion on a newsgroup, disseminate bad advice, and damage the feeling of trust in the newsgroup community. Furthermore, in a group that has become sensitised to trolling—where the rate of deception is high—many honestly naïve questions may be quickly rejected as trollings … Even if the accusation is unfounded, being branded a troll is quite damaging to one's online reputation.[71]*

Yet, it is interesting to note that trolls did not always have the disconcerting label. This ideological package that trolling has assumed came with the Web 2.0 and the interactivity it enabled. Bergstrom explains:

> *Based in Norse mythology, trolls were said to be supernatural creatures with less than benevolent intents. While trolls still make appearances in children's stories and fairy tales, the term "troll" has also taken on a new meaning in our digital age. To be a troll on the Internet is to be much like the Norse trolls, but with less supernatural powers and (perhaps) more malicious intents. When using the term "troll" to describe behaviour online, it often brings with it certain ideological baggage. To troll is to have negative intents, to wish harm or at least discomfort upon one's audience. To be trolled is to be made a victim, to be caught along in the undertow and be the butt of someone else's joke.*

*We are warned "do not feed the troll," as by responding
to their frivolous posts we risk adding fuel to the fire—a
troll is merely looking for any reaction as validation to
continue with their activities.*[72]

Therefore, a troll is someone who frequently posts or engages in inflammatory comments which are often times extraneous or off-topic. Trolls thrive in chat rooms, or social media platforms like Facebook or Twitter. They usually seek to provoke others and seem to take pleasure in doing so. "Trolling is a method of fishing where some baited fishing lines are drawn through the water, usually from a slow-moving boat, with the purpose of hooking unwary fish. An online troll does pretty much the same."[73]

Characteristics of an Internet Troll

A troll has some characteristics that are often employed to inflict chaos on an online network. According to Mehdi,[74] these characteristics are usually but not restricted to the following: using foul language, power of anonymity and an unbridled rage.

Trolls employ foul language, insults and sexual innuendos while trying to prove a point. It does not matter how irrelevant or off-topic their point may be, the troll always has to be arrogantly obtuse.

The internet's basic architecture guarantees anonymity of users. Most social media platforms have gone an extra mile to ensure that the privacy of users is ensured. However, this anonymity grants great comfort to internet trolls. The power of anonymity gives a user within the secluded privacy of safety to tool to inflict vitriol on another user. Many who use uncouth language in their interactions with others may never do so face-to-face to an actual person.

The internet is a neutral tool that has expanded the spaces of conversation. Many times, conversations on social networks also reflect the state of the society. It is therefore not surprising that the anger and frustration that has been inflicted by a society on her citizens is carried into virtual discussions. The troll takes out this frustration on other netizens. The troll makes a whip from unbridled rage and a noose from pent up dissatisfaction.

Twitter Nigeria and the 2015 General Elections

Once upon a time, TwitterNG was peaceful and a pleasant network for political engagement. In the pre-2015 election period, most tweeps were more interested in networking using the social media platforms. This was manifested with TwitterNG as a networked public sphere[75] becoming one of the most influential public spaces in Nigeria. In other words, the once hidden and silent voices had a platform for collective action. One only has to peer into some hashtags that have resonated globally from Nigeria, like #OccupyNigeria or #BringBackOurGirls, to validate this assertion. Whether or not these trends achieved their aim, is a story for another day.

However, as the 2015 elections drew near, the once humane virtual space gradually became toxic. TwitterNG became a space for the battle of supremacy between influential tweeps who sought to win public support – covertly or overtly – for their political candidates and/or parties. This of course made the clime of TwitterNG to become both disruptive and bitter.

The reasons for this interest in the networked public sphere are obvious. The impact of this social media led collective actions in changing the narratives during #OccupyNigeria for instance, was legendary. It thus became obvious to Nigerian politicians that social media, especially Twitter, is a must for anyone that wishes to sell their candidacy or cultivate public goodwill for their government. That obviously is a refreshing perspective, for the once distant "big men/women" of Nigerian politics as they became more accessible to the citizenry. Soon, Twitter morphed from being simply a networked public square into a theatre of political battle.

Trenches soon emerged with very influential Twitter users who decided the agenda of these partisan discourses and got their followers to tweet accordingly. Since these overlords are very powerful persons in the Nigeria Twitter hierarchy, they exercise considerable influence over their followers (voltrons). The voices of the overlords soon became a priced commodity that was rented to support politicians and their parties.

Soon the somewhat calm atmosphere of Twitter

Nigeria was replaced by a combative space characterised by bitter allegiance to either of the two main political parties. This was the background that led to the birth of #TrollCabal.

Making of the #TrollCabal Nigeria

The #TrollCabal started on TwiterNG in 2014. Ikenna Okonkwo (@FailedRift), a geologist, university lecturer, blogger and social media aficionado was the founder and pioneer convener of Twitter Nigeria #TrollCabal. Okonkwo resigned in 2015 and passed on the baton of leadership to Nwachukwu Egbunike (@feathersproject).

This group's aims are entirely non-confessional. #TrollCabal is made up of Nigerian tweeps from diverse ethnic nationalities, political leanings and cultural sympathies. The #TrollCabal gradually swelled to admit many tweeps who desired a break from the bile that characterised conversations on TwitterNG.

Essentially the #TrollCabal makes mockery of the drama that characterises the Nigerian political space. We also mimic the Twitter overlords and their conversations. This takes off the heat which often borders on pure hate. In addition, it provides a counter-narrative that is non-violent and, at the same time, humorous. Hence, Ose Anenih asserts that: "the #TrollCabal is basically an irreverent parody of the Nigerian state. It's a bit of light-hearted fun, but we do try to engage in serious political and social debates devoid of hatred and rancour."[76]

The third convener and the first female to lead the #TrollCabal was Irene Nwaukwa (@cremechic11) who resides in Nairobi, Kenya. The #TrollCabal election was just another way to cool an already inflamed Twitter public sphere. The elections for the leadership of #TrollCabal was held on 19 February 2016. The contestants were: Irene Nwaukwa, Gege (@nigeriabest), who works in the United Kingdom, and Tare Okoro (@tareokoro). The electoral umpire was Kwame Adadevoh (@kwameadadevoh). I think these contestants, the electoral chief and generally Nigerian Twitter users, deserve praise for the conversations that were generated during the elections. For over seventy-two hours before the elections, many tweeps campaigned for their candidates, and even after the elections, the banters continued.

Irene won 51% of the 690 votes and became the third convener on 13 March 2016. The purpose of the election was simply to have fun. The 2016 #TrollCabal elections received wide acceptance and popularity because of its non-confessional and non-partisan stance. Also, the fun was that the same lingo that was deployed during Nigeria's general elections was also adopted by the supporters of each candidate. For instance, tweets like "a major candidate has been arrested, ballot boxes have been snatched or reports of an attempt to rig the elections, and more", were basically what we experienced during the Nigerian general elections.

On 13 March 2017, Ose Anenih (@PapaDonkee)

was sworn in as the fourth convener of the #TrollCabal.[77] Upon assumption of office, Ose appointed Yemi Adesanya (@toyosilagos) as Vice Convener (Papadonkee 2017). "Compared to the immediate past election [2016] which recorded only 690 votes, a total 16, 298 votes were cast [in the 2017 #TrollCabal elections], out of which @Papadonkee got 62% to defeat Jaja – his closest competitor who got 36%."[78] A year later, on 13 March 2018, Jasper J. Weelyams [Jaja] (@JajaPhD) won the elections and took over as the fifth convener of #TrollCabal.

Has the #TrollCabal Nigeria Redefined Trolling?

#TrollCabal is a group of Nigerian Twitter users who resisted the bitter climate of TwitterNG during the 2015 general elections. These tweeps employed humour as a weapon to neutralise the toxic and divisive political conversations around them. Essentially, the #TrollCabal makes mockery of the drama that characterises the Nigerian political space. They also mimic the the conversations of Twitter overlords and the principal political actors in Nigeria. The members of #TrollCabal Nigeria are NOT the usual kind of trolls, with an inherent intent to malign or to unnecessarily hurt people. #TrollCabal are happy and harmless individuals who are committed to providing a more humane climate in reaction to the toxicity around them.

Members of #TrollCabal resisted the vitriol that dominated political discussion on TwitterNG. However, are they different from other trolls? Is their use of "troll"appropriate or is it a metaphor?

Bergstrom argued that a troll may also be one who resists the status quo and gets labeled in the process. Thus, "being labeled as a troll is a way of silencing the transgressor, as well as shutting down debate and self–reflection amongst community members."[79] This means that labelling someone as a troll may be a justification for punishing the person for transgressing community norms. In other words, give a dog a bad name in order to punish it. Stifle dissent by tagging someone who you disagree with as a "troll". This somehow explains the position of the #TrollCabal. They were labeled as disruptors for not joining the fray of partisan bitterness around them. Yet this differs from Bergstrom because the #TrollCabal members were not punished rather they were elected to innovatively change the narrative using humour as a tool.

The irony is that TwitterNG took on all the characteristics that guarantee the thriving of trolls. The political engagement between tweeps, overlords and their voltrons was filled with the weaponisation of foul language. There was a proliferation of handles with no identity and thus used that power of anonymity to inflict unbridled rage on other tweeps. Those who wished to remain unaligned were constantly maligned. The existence of silos of partisan tweeps who propagated the political narrative of their candidates/parties with the most divisive rhetoric became the order of the day. TwitterNG became the real "trolls" while the #TrollCabal provided an antidote to this cruel climate by employing humour as their weapon of trolling.

Also reviewed literature had interrogated the place of identity negotiation with particular emphasis on role-playing.[80]. It is instructive to note that rather than fit into the destructive negative role of the internet troll who escapes from reality by switching to a different online persona, #TrollCabal does exactly the opposite. By insisting on maintaining one persona online and offline, #TrollCabal members seem to have rejected the dualism that have somehow been manifested in literature. The fact is that those who are vile offline have more possibility to transfer that bitterness to their online networks. The converse is also true for those who work to maintain the same personality either online or offline. Therefore, "actual human behaviour online was inextricably interwoven with our offline practices and identities."[81]

Obviously, the real impact of the #TrollCabal on public conversation on Twitter will need a systematic unpacking by media scholars. However, the noon day clarity of the vibrancy of Nigerians on Twitter is one that needs no diviner's peering. The #TrollCabal has blazed the trail in this new conceptualisation of internet trolling. Yomi Adesanya asserts that #TrollCabal is a new sub-culture that promotes social cohesion:

> *The moral dilemma of ensuring inclusivity as well as etiquette in e-deliberations underscores the brilliance of self-identifying as a troll and creating a community of trolls. It is a pragmatic defence of the right of everyone to be heard; an immune system in response to traditional sensibilities threatening to shut up the unruly and the irreverent. #TrollCabal is a sub-culture that is taking root on Twitter, encouraging civil discourse while leaving room for dissent and disputation. By deploying humour and sarcasm, and honing debate and argumentation skills, participants can revel in their freedom of expression and hope to become guardians of liberal democracy. Trolling is being deployed as a tool for social cohesion rather than exclusion: "We all are trolls; now that we got that out of the way, shall we have a meaningful discussion?"[82]*

For once these are trolls with no intention to disrupt, destroy or inflict undue pain. This is a far cry from the battle songs that possessed Nigeria's Twitter-mediated public space. Also, these tweeps saw in the period before the 2015 Nigerian election a capacity for collective action to promote good governance that is non-partisan, non-confessional and has no ethnic label. These factors, unfortunately, have for long saddled political participation in the country.

PART III
ONLINE FREE SPEECH

FREE SPEECH OR FREE SPITE

For a couple of weeks, the world has known no peace as a result of the provocative video thriller—*Innocence of Muslims*. This anti-Islamic film, written and released in 2012, attracted widespread denunciation from Muslims. The said movie went against the tenets of Islam which does not allow any artistic portrayal of the Holy Prophet Mohammed. In addition, this movie produced by Nakoula Basseley Nakoula "is a bigoted piece of poison calculated to inflame the Muslim world. It ought to be treated with the contempt it deserves."[83] Already the rage has consumed John Christopher Stevens, the late US Ambassador to Libya, and many innocent people have been sent on an early and compulsory journey to their graves. At the centre of this crisis, trenches are being dug for and against free speech. What is free speech? Can intentional spite be considered free speech?

No amount of provocation can justify the killing spree and destruction that has characterised the reaction of many of these Muslims. It also goes without saying that just because the movie was made by an irresponsible American does not necessarily mean that the US sponsored or backed the movie. Similarly, it does not mean that all

Christians or Jews are against Muslims. To do so will mean one thing: over-simplifying and amplifying the "single story".

At the same time, no one has the right to castigate other peoples' religion. It is also plain hypocrisy to feign disgust that Muslims are protesting an affront on their religion. As long as it is peaceful, they have a right to protest. After all, people march against other causes. Therein lies the beauty of democracy; if you are not comfortable with an action or inaction, you show your angst by making as much noise as possible—so long as you do not break any law in the process.

Net freedom is founded upon the principles of unfettered freedom of speech. This freedom is uncomfortable for many governments. As such, they try to strangle free speech through legislature, usually citing state security and other reasons. Therefore, the fear of digital freedom is not metaphorical but real. From the Arab Spring, we have ample examples of how politicians tried to cut off voices of their citizens. During the 16 June 1976 Soweto riots, the same happened, but could not repeat itself during the 27 November 2007 strike by the South African miners because of the digital democratisation of information. The genocide in Rwanda was propelled by radio but was well hidden from public glare until late into the massacres. Nonetheless, it is obvious that it would certainly have been more difficult for that to happen in recent times. In 2008, the senate presidents of Nigeria and

Philippines had moved to censor the ubiquitous social media in their respective countries.

However, is free speech absolute? A point of departure is to focus our gaze on man. Human beings are autonomous but not independent. Autonomous in the sense that no two people are the same, and as such, there are no limits to the possibilities inherent in any man. However, man is not totally independent. The grandiose view of man as a being, that is, lord of all, with an unparalleled ability to dominate the world at the expense of others, forms the core of the libertarian mantra. But this self-sufficiency or absolute independence cannot hold true in the face of the infinite needs that each person has: air, water, food, light, friendship, appreciation, love... These are needs that an individual cannot solely acquire alone but must depend on others for maximum satisfaction.

From the foregoing, it means that since man is dependent on others, necessarily his freedom is also limited by other peoples' freedom. Absolute freedom is utopian. Just as governments are required to draw the line during public interventions, especially in trying to gate-keep in the guise of promoting public good; same goes with the individual, who must also draw the line between free speech and free spite.

Hate speech is obviously an abuse of freedom of speech. To accept anything less is to de(i)fy freedom by centralising "i" to deify individual freedom and, in the process, defy other people's freedom. This is particularly pertinent, since we live in a world that sees no reason why the sacred has to be respected. It appears that an unprecedented race is on, where humanity has assumed the right to suffocate the freedom of conscience and religious freedom.

Since no one has been commissioned to take up arms as God's warrior, nonetheless, it is plain clear that there is a sustained and deliberate plan to flare up religious sentiments. It seems the plan is to get the fanatics to draw blood and then turn back to blame religion. The secular and the divine are two separate realms that should remain independent. However, we cannot afford a situation where some—knowing fully well the implications—go ahead to inflame fanatical reactions.

Freedom comes with a corresponding responsibility. There has to be a middle course and knowing when not to lay claim to a "liberty" for the sake of others is plain common sense. A mad French man[84] has added more fuel to an already tense situation. And who will bear the brunt? The innocent, as usual! The fart was released beyond the Atlantic, but the injury will be inflicted down the Sahara; like my fellow citizens who were bombed while worshipping in their church some days ago.

Free spite is not free speech but incendiary rhetoric.

Feathers Project
23 September 2012

GAGGING CRITICS
OR FIGHTING CYBER CRIME?

Nigerian lawmakers are deliberating over multiple bills that aim to fight cybercrime but could gag government critics along the way.

"An Act to Provide for The Prohibition of Electronic Fraud in All Electronic Transactions in Nigeria And for Other Related Matters" [SB198, Year: 2008] would target various forms of fraud and financial crimes[85] carried out online or via mobile phones. Initially sponsored by Ayo Arise, a senator in the 6th National Assembly of Nigeria, the bill's original draft provided long prison terms (of 5 to 14 years) for violators of the law.

The bill's new sponsor, Senator Sefiu Adegbenga Kaka of the 7th National Assembly, has promised to excise "any unacceptable clause(s) in the proposed bill."[86]

This bill's prohibitions on electronic fraud are broadly articulated and cover activities ranging from accessing electronic devices "without authorisation" to "trafficking" passwords:

Prohibition of Electronic Fraud

(1) From the commencement of this Act, no person or corporate body shall:

1. Without authorisation access a computer (or) and other electronic devices or in case of authorisation, exceed authorised access to computers and or communication devices;
2. Use counterfeit access devices;
3. Use unauthorised access devices;
4. Possess any device designed to manipulate credit or ATM card;
5. Damage a government computer with the intent to defraud;
6. Access computer and or electronic device to commit espionage:
7. Traffic in passwords for public, private and or financial institutions computer or relevant electronic devices;
8. Traffic in any password or similar information through which a computer may be accessed without authorisation with intent to defraud, copy financial institutions website, email customers with intention to defraud customers and financial institutions; and
9. Intentionally create computer worms to destroy government computer.

(2) Anybody who contravenes any of the subsections above shall be guilty of an

offence punishable with a sentence of 7 years imprisonment or a fine of 5 million naira, or both.[87]

The section of the bill that has drawn the ire of netizens addresses "false" information:

> **Section 16** (3): Anyone who intentionally propagates false information that could threaten the security of the country or that is capable of inciting the general public against the government through electronic message shall be guilty of a felony, and upon conviction, shall be sentenced to 7 years imprisonment or 5 million Naira fine or both.[88]

Without question, this section of the law could be used to criminalise speech critical of the government. Nevertheless, some influential members of the tech community see value in the measure. Blossom Nnodim, creator of the Adopt-A-Tweep social media and entrepreneurship project, thinks that, "false information" is the operative word in the bill. Nnodim believes that while freedom of speech should be sacrosanct, there must be regulations against defamation or peddling of false news.

The bill could effectively impede Snowden-style

disclosures of classified documents with the following sanctions:

Tampering with Protected Computers

9. From the commencement of this Act, any person who being employed by or under Local, State or Federal Government of Nigeria with respect to working with any protected computer, electronic mails commit any act which he is not authorised to do by virtue of his contract of service or intentionally permits, tampering with such computer, is guilty of a felony and is liable to imprisonment for three years.

Obtaining electronic messages

11. Any person or organisation who by means of false pretence induces the government of Nigeria or any person in charge of electronic devices to deliver to him any electronic messages which includes but is not limited to E-mail messages, credit and debit cards information, facsimile messages which is not specifically meant for him or his organisation (in the latter case except he is authorised to receive such messages for and on behalf of his organisation) is guilty of a misdemeanour and is liable to

imprisonment for two year or a fine of no more than 1 million Naira, or both.[89]

Gbenga Sesan, Executive Director of Paradigm Initiative Nigeria, drew my attention to what he described as a greater potential threat to online freedom in Nigeria— the Cyber Crime Bill (2013)[90]—which is currently at the National Assembly. He also explains why the Cyber Crime Bill is a grave threat to free speech:

> *The new Cyber Crime Bill (2013) has gone through various drafts, including having been known as Cyber Security Bill (2011) at some point. The bill was jointly authored by the… wait for it… National Security Adviser's office and the Ministry of Justice. It had some provisions such as security agents having the power to seize equipment based on reasonable suspicion, but this has since been improved to include the need for a court warrant. The problem with this, in the Nigerian context, is that warrants are easy to obtain since the judiciary isn't exactly an institution that activists or ordinary internet users can rely on. In fact, there's a joke that for the Nigerian judiciary, "the rich get bail, but the poor get jail."[91]*

Sesan fears the bill tips the scales in favour of security agencies and could be used to target voices critical of government online. However, he suspects it may end up on the shelf with 2015 elections not too far off.

This is not the first time Nigeria has come under scrutiny for restrictive internet-related policy-making. In July 2012, we reported on calls from the President of the Nigerian Senate for social media censorship[92]. Earlier this year, we looked into government plans to ramp up internet surveillance[93] using software purchased from Elbit Systems, an Israeli company.

Update [December 11, 2013]: The Nigerian Senate bowed to public criticism and has expunged the offensive section from the proposed bill.

Global Voices Advocacy
10 December 2013

WHY IS ETHIOPIA STRANGLING FREE SPEECH?

Why does a free and vibrant online and offline press pose a threat to the Ethiopian state? Why is Ethiopia on this self-destructive race to assume the number one position as the enemy of free speech on the African continent? When did it become a crime to be a journalist, to preach the truth and serve it to all? One cannot but ask these questions following the recent arrest of six members of *Zone9 Bloggers Collective* in a country reputed to be the cradle of humanity.

Ethiopia has a repressible history of stifling free speech. Reeyot Alemu—a columnist and English school teacher—and four other journalists, were arrested in 2011, and convicted based on a trumped-up charge of terrorism. The other journalists are Woubshet Taye, Eskinder Nega, Yusuf Getachew and Solomon Kebede.

Eskinder Nega, journalist and blogger, was given an 18-year jail sentence under the Ethiopian anti-terror law. Nega's crime was voicing his opposition in an article against government's silencing of vocal critics. Mr Nega was awarded the 2014 Golden Pen of Freedom.

The grave injustice and threat to the most fundamental rights are being abused in the most flagrant manner in

Ethiopia. It has never been an easy task to be a journalist anywhere on this planet, however, it seems that to be a journalist or blogger in Ethiopia automatically translates into a death sentence. Sadly, the African Union plays the ostrich while the Ethiopian government morphs into a rabid predator of free speech.

Free speech is on trial in Ethiopia; it is not simply a matter of strangling press freedom. Rather Ethiopia has taken the sloppy path of killing any form of dissent. The social media is the newest victim in this deliberate and systemic plan to gag Ethiopians forever. Having sealed the fate of traditional journalists, the government is now set for a major crackdown on their online counterparts – the Bloggers of Zone9 (*see* "The Campaign to #FreeZone9Bloggers"). It is doubly painful that the very essence of a free web is being challenged in the twenty-first century yet, only very few seem to care. There is no excuse for the deadly silence of the continent's mainstream media on this grave assault. None whatsoever!

African Hadithi
30 April 2014

BEFEQADU HAILU, AN ETHIOPIAN WRITER IN CHAINS!

Befeqadu Hailu, is a thirty-five-year-old writer that could not deaden his conscience to state brutality on free speech. An award-winning novelist—2012 third place winner of the Burt Award for African Literature—and poet, it was not surprising that his passion found visible expression in blogging and co-founding of the "Zone9 Bloggers Collective".

Using the internet, Befeqadu personified those eternal words of the grandfather of African Literature, Chinua Achebe: "An artist, in my understanding of the word, should side with the people against the Emperor that oppresses his or her people." And for doing this, Befeqadu is currently in chains.

Befeqadu and eight others have been charged with terrorism and have been incarcerated since April 2014. But the real terrorists are Befeqadu's jailers; a repressive government that does not condone critical dissent. That is indeed Befeqadu and his colleagues' greatest crime—refusing to "conform" to the norm of silence. This trait is obviously innate in any writer; the compulsion not to keep quiet. The poetry in Befeqadu's veins could not be bottled up by state terror, nor stifled by jail bars.

Writing from prison, Befeqadu's strong and unbending will to stand for the truth remains unbroken:

"So, what do you think is your crime?"

The question is intriguing. It sheds light on our innocence and on our refusal to acknowledge whatever crimes our captors suspect us of committing. Yes, they probed us severely, but each session ends with the same question. The investigation was not meant to prove or disprove our offences. It was meant simply to make us plead guilty.

After two years of writing and working to engage citizens in a political debate, we have been apprehended and investigated. Blame is being laid upon us for committing criminal acts, for supposedly being members and "accepting the missions" of [opposition political parties] ...[94]

The weight of that question: "so what do you think is your crime?" and the corresponding response sheds light on the irony of the jailer (who is in captivity of fear) and the jailed (who possesses interior freedom). In the words of Wole Soyinka, "books and all forms of writing are terror to those who wish to suppress the truth."

Weaving stories untold
Lauding stories unheard
Shouting for gagged voices
Serving rising voices
From the four-compass point
From the sun rising to its setting
From the Atlantic to the Sahara
Let a mighty echo arise, #FreeZone9Bloggers!

Global Voices Advocacy
5 June 2015

THE CAMPAIGN TO #FREEZONE9BLOGGERS OF ETHIOPIA

In April 2014, six bloggers and three journalists were arrested in Ethiopia. The six Ethiopians bloggers are members of Zone9 (a collective blog) that covered social and political issues and promoted human rights and government accountability in the country.

The six arrested bloggers are Abel Wabella, Atnaf Berhane, Mahlet Fantahun, Natnail Feleke, Zelalem Kibret and Befekadu Hailu; while the three journalists are: Asmamaw Hailegeorgis, Tesfalem Waldyes and Edom Kassaye. Four of the Zone9 bloggers were my colleagues, *Global Voices* contributors who worked to build the Global Voices Amharic, a language widely spoken in Ethiopia. In July of the same year, they were charged under the country's Anti-Terrorism Proclamation[95] and accused of "working with foreign organisations that claim to be human rights activists and…receiving finance to incite public violence through social media."[96]

"We Cannot Remain Silent"

Global Voices (GV), is an international online community of "bloggers, journalists, translators, academics and human right activists that leverage on the power of the internet to build understanding across borders."[97] GV achieves this ambitious objective by relying on its network of eight hundred contributors in thirty countries to report news that hardly make headlines in mainstream media; translate these posts into many languages and defend online free speech. Advox (Global Voices Advocacy) is a project of GV that is dedicated to reporting "threats to online speech, share tactics for defending the work and words of netizens, and support efforts to improve Internet policy and practice worldwide."[98]

The #Zone9 Bloggers were contributors and translators for GV. Hence, their arrest resonated deeply within our community.

> *Since 2012, the Zone 9 blogging collective has worked to foster civic engagement and critical commentary about social and political issues in Ethiopia. Despite difficult conditions, they have exercised their right to free expression in the interest of promoting peaceful dialogue and debate. Global Voices is a community bloggers, activists, writers, and translators from 137 countries. The universal human right to free expression is fundamental to our mission: to tell underreported stories from around the world and defend the rights of everyone to speak freely and without fear. We are outraged by this flagrant violation of our friends' rights to free expression and deeply concerned for their safety. We cannot remain silent.[99]*

The above statement was translated into over fifteen languages: Dutch, French, Malagasy, Portuguese, Spanish, Polish, Catalan, and others. Many other posts also kept track of the plight of the jailed #Zone9 bloggers. However, at a point we had to re-innovate our strategy.

Naturally, it is one thing to protect online free speech of others, but certainly a different thing altogether to demand for the right to freedom of one's colleagues. The cycle of hope and anguish; the despair that comes with waiting and waiting with no news. That burnout that slowly creeps in due to that nagging thought that you have not done enough or that all these efforts do not matter or even worse, will amount to nothing. These are sentiments that can never be fully captured by human rights activists who have worked to demand the freedom of others. However, in the succeeding paragraphs, I will present two impactful #FreeZone9bloggers campaigns that I initiated and was promoted by Advox during the period of their incarceration.

"They Have Names Series"

The *Global Voices* community and the Sub-Sahara African team in particular, worked hard for over the past twelve months of the arrest and jailing of #Zone9 bloggers. We drew global attention to their case and celebrated the contributions of these brave Ethiopians to online discourse. Nonetheless, as it usually happens with most campaigns, the message reaches a saturation point where the victims become just mere statistics. With the then prevailing political situation in Ethiopia, the government cracked down on any form of dissent and sent many activists to prison.

Therefore, we had to come up with a more innovative approach to keep the plight of our colleagues in global headlines. In these circumstances, my disposition as a poet and my African worldview came in handy. I suggested that we highlight each individual blogger with a special piece of writing, art, poetry or video. This was how the "They have Names Series" was born.

They have Names—they are not just numbers! These nine Ethiopians were unjustly hooded into jail by those who have been entrusted with the common good. We will recount their stories in the weeks to come. What's in a name? The very essence of one's humanity. The African worldview holds that names cannot be erased. However, a tyrannical state wishes to do just that.

The *Zone9* bloggers' crime was that they dared to live out "Ubuntu". They promoted their community above individualistic concerns. Their work was to push and tear down the large barriers of the proverbial "Zone Nine" prison of Ethiopia. Freedom is on trial; free speech is dead. The silence of fear is alive.

Using the Internet, these men and women expanded the zone of freedom. But as a reward, they were inflicted with trumped-up terrorism charges. It only made sense that we (the Global Voices Advocacy Sub-Saharan African team) had to keep these names alive and tell their tale of courage for all to hear using the internet. We had to prevent a reductionist approach of counting them merely as numbers or as martyrs. They have names, stories, personalities, quirks, flaws.

Names, stories
Zoned into gaol
Nine not none
Gagged not mute
Suppressed not erased.

The First African Tweetathonto #FreeZone9Bloggers

A tweetathon is a Twitter campaign; it is like an online marathon. The main objective is to trend a hashtag. Thus, it is imperative that for a tweetathon to be successful and have the desired impact, it has to resonate for a long period. This implies that the hashtag has to be tweeted by a large number of people and also by influential tweeps for the desired outcome to occur.

Hence, I proposed to Hisham Almiraat (former Advox director), Ellery Roberts Bridle (then editor of Advox) and Ndesanjo Macha (Tanzanian contributor and former Sub Sahara African editor of Global Voices) to organise an African Tweetathon to #FreeZone9Bloggers. As soon as they bought into the idea, I invited Blossom Ozurumba (formerly Nnodim) an influential Nigerian tweep to join the team.

126

Join Nigerian bloggers Blossom Nnodim (@blcompere) and Nwachukwu Egbunike (@feathersproject), along with Global Voices editor Ndesanjo Macha (@ndesanjo) from Tanzania for an Africa-wide tweetathon in support of the nine bloggers and journalists arrested in late April and currently being detained in Ethiopia… This Wednesday, beginning at 2 p.m. West African Time, we plan to tweet at community leaders, government and diplomatic actors, and mainstream media (using their handles) to increase awareness and draw public attention to the case. We especially encourage fellow bloggers and social media users in Africa to join us—but anyone is welcome.[100]

Blossom was indeed a providential addition to our team. She brought to bear on this campaign her vast experience in digital advocacy "social media for social good"[101] on this campaign. For instance, the decision on the time of the tweetathon was a manifestation of Blossom's competence and contextual understanding of TwitterNG. She suggested that we start the tweetathon by 2 p.m. West African time. This is because by the time the campaign gains traction, it will coincide with peak time in TwitterNG. We then set about to produce a manual and online banner for the tweetathon.

The African Tweetathon calling for the release of the nine jailed Ethiopian bloggers took place on 14 May

2014. Due to the success of the African led campaign, we decided to host a Multilingual Global Tweetathon by taking advantage of the diversity of the Global Voices community, to tweet the #FreeZone9Bloggers hashtag from different time zones and in diverse languages on 4 August 2014.

Nigerian writer and GV community leader Nwachukwu Egbunike responded to the call with zeal. "Something just occurred to me," he wrote to our mailing list. "The last Twitter Campaign was led by Anglophone Africa but had a global impact. Can we have a truly global campaign this time around, tweeting in various languages at a specific time for the #Zone9Bloggers? At least for starters: English, French and Portuguese Africa calling for their release, same day, same time with same hashtag!" After a few days of organising local teams in as many time zones as we could cover—from Hong Kong to Islamabad to Cairo to San Francisco—a global, multilingual tweetathon was born. Nwachukwu helped kick things off with a series of inspiring tweets for our global community. This is one of the tweets: Egbunike, Nwachukwu (@feathersproject). "Though tongues may differ, yet with many tongues we raise a mighty clamour for our common humanity, #FreeZone9Bloggers." 31 July 2014, 9:41 a.m. Tweet.[102]

Both campaigns were successful and trended globally on Twitter and Tumblr[103] for many days and the # hashtag was tweeted more than eight thousand times. It was also picked up by mainstream media. Endalk and I were interviewed by the Voice of America after the multilingual tweetathon.

> *The arrests stirred a high profile international social media campaign to free the arrested bloggers, which spread online behind the #FreeZone9Bloggers hashtag. The popularity of the campaign was unprecedented in Ethiopia. After its launch, the campaign gained visibility internationally, including the first African-wide "tweetathon" organised in solidarity by Nigerian and Tanzanian bloggers, and legal petitions addressed to the African Union and the United Nations' Human Rights Council.* [104]

These Global Voices campaigns irked the Ethiopian government because of the systematic and sustained international attention that we gave to the call to #FreeZone9Bloggers. One of us, a Ghanaian, attended a conference organised by an African Union agency in Addis Ababa during the period of intense campaign. He was almost arrested at the airport because his name was on the list of "enemies" of the government. It took the concerted effort of the AU officials to get the secret service officials of Ethiopia off his back. This Ghanaian's only "crime" was that he wrote for Global Voices.

This does not include the unending hate mails that many of us received. Endalk Chala, a member of the Zone9 and writer for Global Voices, was the most hit by this endless psychological harassment from Ethiopian trolls. Endalk was lucky to have migrated to the United States for postgraduate studies before the onslaught on free speech began with vehement vengeance in Ethiopia. Thus, he had the singular privilege to provide the nuanced context that was imperative in telling the Ethiopian story to the world. Endalk translated most of the posts from Amharic to English and was instrumental in keeping in contact with our incarcerated Zone9 friends. However, this came at a price: Endalk endured the most agonising vitriol from agents of the Ethiopian state including death threats. This is in addition to the ever-present guilt of being separated from friends during their greatest agony.

Other unsung protagonists of this campaign are Ndesanjo Macha and Ellery Roberts Bridle. Ndesanjo was one of the pioneers of blogging in East Africa both in English and Swahili. He had an extensive network that came in handy during the #FreeZone9Bloggers. Ellery was a significant help during those dark days. An American of Cuban origin, Ellery's focus in scholarship and practice was on advocacy, surveillance and internet governance. Her breath, scope, understanding and empathy during the #FreeZone9Bloggers campaign was legendary. If a content analysis was to be done on the number of stories that were published, initiated and/or promoted about the jailed Zone9 bloggers across many platforms – traditional and digital – Ellery's byline will certainly take the first place.

Of course, the Global Voices community as a whole takes the greatest commendation. This amazing community of translators, writers and human rights activists put in their all, individually and as a group. Many GVers aside taking part in the campaigns enumerated above also protested before the embassy of Ethiopia in their various countries. They mobilised their friends and colleagues to sign letters of petition to various international human right bodies domiciled in their respective countries.

In July 2015, our Ethiopian friends regained their freedom after spending eighteen months in jail. Those released were Tesfalem Waldyes, Asmamaw Hailegiorgis; and three Zone9 bloggers: Zelalem Kiberet, Mahlet Fantahun and Edom Kassaye; along with Ethiopian journalist, Reeyot Alemu.[104] Later that year, on 16 October, four others of Zone9 – Soliana Shimelis, Atnaf Berhane, Abel Wabella and Natnail Feleke – had their charges dropped and they were acquitted and discharged.[105]

It was indeed an unmerited privilege to have worked with this impressive team during the #FreeZone9Bloggers campaign. Indeed, evil only triumphs when good people keep silent!

APPENDIX

APPENDIX

#BRINGBACKOURGIRLS: STATEMENT FROM CONCERNED NIGERIAN BLOGGERS

We, the undersigned Nigerian bloggers, view with grave concern the continued detention of the innocent school girls who were abducted from Chibok on 15 April 2014.

We are of the strong view that no amount of social grievance, either against the government, and, or the people of Nigeria can justify such an act of violence against school children. We therefore condemn the abduction in very strong terms.

Nonetheless, we are appalled that despite the increasing global attention on the missing girls, there seems to be relative local press silence on it.

In addition, we have also noticed gaps in the narrative on this incident, both on social media platforms, and in the international press. It is understandable that given the strong emotions that this abduction has evoked, accurate and fact-based narratives are difficult to come by on this sad incidence of violence.

We wish to point out that the abduction and continued absence of these innocent school girls violates the provisions of a number of international conventions, optional protocols of conventions and international legal instruments to which Nigeria is a signatory to and whose provisions bind all Nigerians.

We particularly call attention to those international conventions that enjoin parties in conflict to take special action to protect women and children in times of war and conflict and note that the abduction is an affront to these provisions and to every decent conduct.

We call on the abductors to kindly release our girls. We appeal to you in the name of God and all that you hold dear.

We deplore the violence and loss of lives that have preceded this ugly event and urge you in name of God who is a God of peace, reconciliation and forgiveness, to embrace the path of dialogue as the only sure way of resolving the grievances that underlie this conflict. May the God of peace and compassion touch your hearts and make you hearken to this appeal from your fellow citizens.

We also call on the government of Nigeria to do everything in its power, even if it includes involving an international security agency, to bring the girls back from the hands of those who currently hold them and restore a sense of security to the country as soon as possible. Elections are coming up next year. Citizens want to feel safe wherever they are. Democracy thrives best when citizens feel empowered to pursue their daily chores without fear or threat to their lives and property.

This statement is endorsed by the following:

Nwachukwu Egbunike: (@feathersproject) *Feathersproject. wordpress.com*

Ikenna Okonkwo: (@failedrift) *Failedrift.wordpress.com*

Kola Tubosun: (@baroka) *KTravula.com*

Olumide Abimbola: (@loomnie) *NigeriansTalk.com*

Noel Ihebuzor: (@naitwt) *Voicevisionandviews.wordpress. com*

Mark Amaza: (@amasonic) *markamaza.com*

Sylva Nze Ifedigbo: (@nzesylva) *nzesylva.wordpress.com*

Ayodele Olofintuade: (@aeolofintuade) *Totallyhawaya-haywire.blogspot.com*

4 May 2014

ETHNIC HATE SPEECH: STATEMENT FROM CONCERNED NIGERIAN WRITERS

We, the undersigned Nigerian writers, view with grave concern the dominance of ethnic incendiary speech in our country. We are deeply troubled that the public space—both online and offline—has been hijacked by a vocal minority of individuals who promote ethnocentric ideas inimitable to the peace and wellbeing of a majority of citizens. Nigerian citizens have a right to freely express their opinions on governance as enshrined in the Constitution. However, this fundamental right to freedom of speech is being used to disseminate hate speech, which goes contrary to the right itself and the spirit of the Constitution that enshrines it.

Nigeria is a federated state with over two hundred and fifty ethnic groups and five hundred languages. The survival of our one hundred and seventy million people lies in our ability to curtail conflicting ethnic tensions. We have, however, had instances of conflict along ethno-religious lines, most notably the Civil War in the period 1967 to 1970 which saw millions of Nigerian citizens killed. The "us" against "them" rhetoric that ignited bloodshed of a bestial magnitude since independence has re-surfaced again. A new breed of ethnic entrepreneurs seems hell-bent on causing anarchy for political motives. The lessons of our history are being ignored. Strength in diversity is considered weakness.

We, as writers, are aware of the effects of such parochial politics on our continent: the ethnic tensions in the early 1970s in Zambia, the animus of ethnic hate in post-apartheid South Africa, the horrors of the Rwandan genocide, the ongoing displacement and insecurity in Burundi and parts of the Democratic Republic of Congo, the post-election ethnic killings in Kenya, are warning markers of note.

We strongly believe that no amount of social grievance against the government can justify this level of irresponsible ethnocentric hatred currently being peddled by a growing number of disgruntled groups across the country. Similarly, we are mortified by the initial nonchalance and apparent misguided handling by the authorities of the root cause of hate speech in the country.

We condemn this growing trend of hate speech in the strongest terms.

Freedom of speech, though sacrosanct, is not absolute. Our freedom is a shared one, limited by the freedom of others. Citizens must draw the line between free speech and arbitrary spite. For a multi-ethnic state with fault lines such as ours, the lasting solution lies in healing the cleavages that promote ethnic division. This also means the triumph of a national identity that transcends the opportunistic ethnocentric group identity, which has been the bane of Nigeria's nationhood. Clearly, we cannot pretend that all is well with our "federation". We assert that our union can only be saved by transparency, frankness and a deliberate revision of structures and relations. Because of the lack of boldness and the inactions of the past, we have a bad deal of a leprous nation in our hands. As writers, we insist, that there should be no prevarication in this matter. We reiterate the call for the restructuring of Nigeria in a manner of true federalism.

We also call on the government of Nigeria to do everything in its power to protect her citizens and avert another spate of useless killings, and to listen to all aggrieved segments in a constructive and productive manner. It is the duty of government to make the country livable just as it is for citizens to work in building a country to which we are all happy to belong. This means an interrogation of our national memory, reinstating the teaching of a thorough curriculum of Nigerian history in primary and secondary schools, a celebration of our individual cultures and languages, and, above all, the application of justice where rights have been violated.

Nigeria's democracy, attained through great sacrifice and loss, now faces its most crucial test of ensuring that citizens are safe wherever they choose to reside, be it in the north-east, north-west, north-central, south-east, south-west, or south-south.

Thus, we condemn hate speech or ethnic-based politics or activism that seeks to challenge the right of

Nigerians to live, work, or associate in peace anywhere in the country. We also call on all Nigerians to unite and face our common enemies—those who have sworn to destroy our common wealth. We stand for open association, peaceful engagement and the nurturing of diversity. In insisting on this, we, as writers, stand for a secure country with a just society worthy of all our aspirations.

Signed:
Nwachukwu Egbunike
Kola Tubosun
Ikhide R. Ikheloa
Chiagozie Fred Nwonwu
Niran Okewole
Tade Ipadeola
Richard Ali
Abubakar Adam Ibrahim
Servio Gbadamosi
Su'eddie Vershima Agema
Sylva Nze Ifedigbo
Tope Folarin
Tunde Leye
Uchenna Ekwerenmadu
Remi Raji
Ropò Ewénlá
Ikenna Ndu
Dami Ajayi
Ayodele Olofintuade

Chika Unigwe
Abimbola Adunni Adelakun
Ukamaka Olisakwe
Eghosa Imasuen
Temitayo Olofinlua
Terseer Sam Baki
Femi Morgan
Jumoke Verissimo
Echezonnachukwu Nduka

28 June 2017

REFERENCES

1. Internetlivestats (2016). Retrieved from http://www.inter-netlivestats.com/internet-users/nigeria/

2. Alexis (2016). Retrieved from http://www.alexa.com/topsites/countries/NG.

3. "A World of Connections: A Special Report on Social Networking," *The Economist*. 28 January 2010.

4. Mbalo, C. (2015). "Facebook Mobile Use Statistics in Africa (Nigeria leads in number of users). *A Nairobian's Perspective!*" 10 September 2015, http://siku-moja.blogspot.com.ng/2015/09/facebook-mobile-use-statistics-in.html#. Vw0cPTArLIU

5. Portlands, How Africa tweets. 2016. Retrieved from http://www.howafricatweets.com/

6. Granello, D. H., and Wheaton, J. E., "Online Data Collection: Strategies for Research," *Journal of Counseling and Development, 82* no.4 (2004): 387-393.

7. Skågeby, J., "Online Ethnographic Methods: Towards a Qualitative Understanding of Virtual Community Practices," in Daniel, B. K. (Ed)'s *Handbook of Research on Methods and Techniques for Studying Virtual Communities: Paradigms and Phenomena* Hershey PA: IGI Global, USA, (2011): 410-428.

8. Bowler, G. M., "Netnography: A Method Specifically Designed to Study Cultures and Communities Online," *The Qualitative Report: Fort Lauderdale* 15, no.5 (Sept. 2010): 1270-1275.

9. Burbidge, D., "Can Someone Get Me Outta this Middle-Class Zone?!: Pressures of Middle Class Kikuyu in Kenya's 2013 Elections," *Journal of Modern African Studies* 52, no. 2, (June 2014): 205-225.

10. Weber, C., "Emotions, campaigns and political participation," *Political Research Quarterly* 66, no. 2 (June 2013): 414-425

11. Internetlivestats. Retrieved on 12 April 2016 from http://www.internetlivestats.com/internet-users/nigeria/

12. Egbunike, N. A and Nwogwugwu, D. I., "The management of social media campaign in Nigeria's presidential election, case study of a Nigerian political party," in press, in *Social Media, Political Participation and the Consolidation of Democracy in Nigeria*, ed. Alaki, A. O. & Eke, K. K (Lexington Books: an imprint of Rowman & Littlefield).

13. Egbunike N. A, Ihebuzor N. and Onyechi N., "Nature of Tweets in the 2015 Nigerian Presidential Elections," *International Journal of Civic Engagement and Social Change* 2 no.2 (April-June 2015): 34-52.

14. Independent National Electoral Commission, "Presidential Election Summary of Results," 28 March 2015. Retrieved from http://www.inecnigeria.org/wp-content/uploads/2015/04/summary-of-results.pdf

15. Samuel Ogundipe, "Buhari govt. has let me down, pro-APC blogger says after regaining freedom," *Premium Times*, 10 August 2016. Retrieved from: https://www.premiumtimesng.com/news/more-news/208355-buhari-govt-let-pro-apc-blogger-says-regaining-freedom.html

16. Endalk Chala, "Ethiopia locks down digital communications in wake of #OromoProtests," *Global Voices*, 14 July 2016. https://globalvoices.org/2016/07/14/ethiopia-locks-down-digital-communications-in-wake-of-oromoprotests/

17. Ndesanjo Macha, "Calls for the International Community to Intervene as Gambia Continues to Imprison Dissidents," *Global Voices*, 24 July 2016. Retrieved from: https://globalvoices.org/2016/07/24/calls-for-the-international-community-to-intervene-as-gambia-continues-to-imprison-dissidents/

18. Ndesanjo Macha, "'Uganda Is a Boiling Pot': Arrests, Rigging Claims and a Social Media Shutdown Mar Elections," *Global Voices,* 20 February 2016. Retrieved from: https://globalvoices.org/2016/02/20/uganda-is-a-boiling-pot-arrests-rigging-claims-and-a-social-media-shutdown-mar-elections/

19. Netizen Report, "Uganda and Nigeria seek stricter controls for social media," *Global Voices Advocacy*, 16 March 2016. Retrieved from: https://globalvoices.org/2016/03/16/netizen-report-uganda-and-nigeria-seek-stricter-controls-for-social-media/

20. Premium Times, "Editorial: The menace called 'Radio Biafra,'" *Premium Times*, 10 July 2015. Retrieved from: https://www.premiumtimesng.com/opinion/editorial/186424-editorial-the-menace-called-radio-biafra.html

21. Amoskalu, "Is Nigeria Really a Zoo? – According to Buhari and Kanu," *CNN iReport*, 18 November 2015. Retrieved from: http://ireport.cnn.com/docs/DOC-1283334

22. Chika Ebuzor, "IPOB leader explains why he called Nigeria a zoo," *PulseNG*, 5 January 2016. Retrieved from: http://www.pulse.ng/news/local/nnamdi-kanu-ipob-leader-explains-why-he-called-nigeria-a-zoo-id4522704.html

23. Kemisola Adeyemi, "The emergence of Radio Biafra and the Hate Speech – 'I'll Kill Deeeper Life's Pastor Kumuyi,'" *Kemi-filani Blog*, 25 June 2015. Retrieved from: https://www.kemi-filani.com/2015/06/the-emergence-of-radio-biafra-and-hate.html

24. Sahara Reporters, "Buhari's Statement at the US Institute of Peace that made everyone cringe," Sahara Reporters, 25 July 2015. Retrieved from: http://saharareporters.com/2015/07/25/buhari%E2%80%99s-statement-us-institute-peace-made-every-one-cringe-0

25. The Punch, "Editorial: Buhari's parochial appointments," *The Punch*, 1 August 2016. Retrieved from: http://punchng.com/bu-haris-parochial-appointments/

26. Sahara Reporters, "Northern youths declare war on Igbos in the north, ask them to 'leave' within three months," *Sahara Reporters*, 6 June 2017. Retrieved from: http://saharareporters.com/2017/06/06/northern-youths-declare-war-igbos-north-ask-them-%E2%80%98leave%E2%80%99-within-three-months

27. Omotayo Yusuf, "Niger Delta reacts to quit notice issued by Arewa youths to Igbos," *NAIJ.com*. Retrieved from: https://www.naija.ng/1108819-niger-delta-reacts-quit-notice-issued-by-are-wa-youths-igbos.html#1108819

28. Lasse Heerten and A. Dirk Moses, "The Nigeria–Biafra war: postcolonial conflict and the question of genocide," *Journal of Genocide Research 16*, no. 2 -3, (21 August 2014): 169-203.

29. Osaghae, E. E. and Suberu, R. T., "A history of identities, violence, and stability in Nigeria," *CRISE Working Paper*, No. 6 (January 2005): 8.

30. Egbunike N. A, Ihebuzor N. and Onyechi N., "Nature of Tweets in the 2015 Nigerian Presidential Elections," *International Journal of Civic Engagement and Social Change 2*, no. 2 (April – June): 34-52.

31. Egbunike N. A and Ihebuzor N., "Online ethnocentrism and Nigerian youths," in press, *New Media and Society*.

32. Egbunike N. A. and Onyechi N. J., "Facebooking ethnicity in the political storytelling of Nigerians," *Journal of Communication and Language Art 7*, no. 1 (2016): 21-42.

33. Sahara Reporters, "Buhari returns to Nigeria after medical vacation in London," 2016. Retrieved from: http://saharareporters.com/photos/photonews-buhari-returns-nigeria-after-medical-vacation-london

34. Isiaka Wakili, "Transcript of President Buhari's Speech: Nigeria's Unity Settled," *Sahara Reporters,* 21 August 2017. Retrieved from: http://saharareporters.com/2017/08/21/transcript-president-buharis-speech-nigeria%E2%80%99s-unity-settled

35. Pius Okigbo III, "I am a Nigerian, pure and simple, but I do not agree that 'Nigeria's unity has been settled and is not negotiable...,'" Facebook, 21 August 2017. Retrieved from: https://www.facebook.com/patrick.okigboiii/posts/10213908681372867

36. Reuben Abati, "The Nnamdi Kanu phenomenon," *Sahara Reporters,* 5 July 2017. Retrieved from: http://saharareporters.com/2017/07/05/nnamdi-kanu-phenomenon-reuben-abati

37. Ikeogwu Oke, "I have read—and reread—the latest speech by President Buhari. I agree that it could be improved, like any other speech...," Facebook, 22 August 2017. Retrieved from: https://www.facebook.com/ikeogu/posts/10212874010659192?pnref=story.unseen-section

38. Mazi Nwonwu, "Did any of you read *Divided We Stand* by the gifted Ekwensi? It is a forerunner of Chimamanda Ngozi Adichie's Half of a Yellow Sun…," Facebook, 22 August 2017. Retrieved from: https://www.facebook.com/fred.c.nwonwu/posts/10211904082171407

39. Ayatse, F. H and Akuva, I. I., "The Origin and development of ethnic politics and its impacts on post-colonial governance in Nigeria," *European Scientific Journal (ESJ)* 9, no. 17 (2013).

40. Clay Shirky, "The Political Power of Social Media," *Foreign Affairs*, January/February. 2011. Retrieved from: https://www.foreignaffairs.com/articles/2010-12-20/political-power-social-media

41. *Ibid*.

42. Barassi, V., "Digital vs. Material: The Everyday Construction of Mediated Political Action," *Networking Knowledge: Journal of the MeCCSA Postgraduate Network* 1, no. 2 (2009).

43. Scan News, "Boko Haram leader claims responsibility for Lagos, Abuja explosions," 14 July 2014. Retrieved from: https://scannewsnigeria.com/news/boko-haram-leader-claims-responsibility-for-lagos-abuja-explosions/

44. Nwogwugwu, D.; Egbunike, N. A.; Ajayi, T; Lawal, A; Salako, Y. and Olanipekun, T., *Rebranding Nigeria*, an MA PR Group Presentation, Department of Communication and Language Arts, University of Ibadan (unpublished), (2013).

45. Scheufele, D. A and Tewksbury, D., "Framing, Agenda Setting and Priming: The Evolution of Three Media Effects Models," *Journal of Communication* 57 (2007): 9-20.

46. World Health Organisation, "Nigeria is now free of Ebola virus transmission. Ebola situation assessment," 20 October 2014. Retrieved from: http://www.who.int/mediacentre/news/ebola/20-october-2014/en/

47. Nwachukwu Egbunike, "With doctors on strike and Boko Haram on the loose, Nigerians fear an Ebola outbreak," *Global Voices*, 29 July 2014. Retrieved from: https://globalvoices.org/2014/07/29/liberian-man-infected-with-ebola-dies-lagos-nigeria/

48. Katherine Harmon Courage, "How Did Nigeria Quash Its Ebola Outbreak So Quickly?" *Scientific America*, 18 October 2014. Retrieved from: https://www.scientificamerican.com/article/how-did-nigeria-quash-its-ebola-outbreak-so-quickly/

49. Centers for Disease Control, "Ebola Virus Disease Outbreak—Nigeria," *Weekly 63,* no. 39 (October 3 2014): 867-872. Retrieved from: https://www.cdc.gov/mmwr/preview/mmwrhtml/mm6339a5.htm?s_cid=mm6339a5_w)

50. Amnesty International, "Nigeria: Massacre possibly deadliest in Boko Haram's history," Press Release, 9 January 2015. Retrieved from: https://www.amnesty.org/en/press-releases/2015/01/nigeria-massacre-possibly-deadliest-boko-haram-s-history/

51. Kim Willsher, Jon Henley, Anne Penketh and Luke Harding, "A ruthless enemy, hostages and trail of murder: France's worst nightmare," *The Guardian*, 9 January 2015. Retrieved from: https://www.theguardian.com/world/2015/jan/09/charlie-hebdo-attack-brothers-killed-police-hostages-jewish-supermarket

52. Ethan Zukerman, "Media coverage of Charlie Hebdo and the Baga massacre: a study in contrasts," *The Conversation*, 13 January 2015. Retrieved from: https://theconversation.com/media-coverage-of-charlie-hebdo-and-the-baga-massacre-a-study-in-contrasts-36225

53. Simon Allison, "I am Charlie, but I am Baga too: On Nigeria's forgotten massacre," *Daily Maverick*, 12 January 2015. Retrieved from: https://www.dailymaverick.co.za/article/2015-01-12-i-am-charlie-but-i-am-baga-too-on-nigerias-forgotten-massacre/#.WzCucadKjIW

54. BBC, "Boko Haram crisis: Nigerian archbishop accuses West," 12 January 2015. Retrieved from: https://www.bbc.com/news/world-africa-30777066

55. AIT, "President Jonathan flays attack on French magazine," 2015. Retrieved from: http://aitonline.tv/post-president_jonathan_flays_attack_on_french_magazine

56. Encomium, "President Jonathan visits Nigerian soldiers in Maiduguri, salutes their courage and patriotism," 15 January 2015. Retrieved from: http://encomium.ng/president-jonathan-visits-nigerian-soldiers-in-maiduguri-salutes-their-courage-and-patriotism/

57. Jeremy Adam Smith, "The first thing you'll notice is that there is not a lot of coverage of the massacres in Baga and Askira; in many papers, it's totally unmentioned and invisible...," Facebook, 13 January 2015. Retrieved from: https://www.facebook.com/jeremyadamsmith/posts/10205153768820477

58. Cohen, Mike, and Yinka Ibuken, "After Nigeria election win, Buhari targets Boko Haram, graft," *Bloomberg Business*, 2 April 2015. Retrieved from: http://www.bloomberg.com/news/articles/2015-04-02/after-nigerian-election-win-buhari-targets-boko-haram-graft

59. Nwachukwu Egbunike, "Nigeria: Social Media and the 2011 Elections," *Global Voices*, 4 May 2011. Retrieved from: https://globalvoices.org/2011/05/04/nigeria-social-media-and-the-2011-elections/

60. Lauren Said-Moorhouse, "Win it like Buhari: 5 startup lessons to take away from Nigerian elections," *CNN*, 9 April 2015. Retrieved from: https://edition.cnn.com/2015/04/09/africa/startup-lessons-nigerian-election-buhari-campaign/index.html

61. Vanguard, "Read President Buhari's inaugural speech on 29 May 2015," Retrieved from: https://www.vanguardngr.com/2015/05/read-president-buhari-inaugural-speech/

62. Nwachukwu Egbunike, "Nigeria: BattaBox bakes stories through online videos," *Global Voices*, 14 May 2012. Retrieved from: https://globalvoices.org/2012/05/14/nigeria-battabox-bakes-stories-through-online-videos/

63. Nwachukwu Egbunike, "Why I choose to sit on the fence," *The Scoop*, 12 January 2015. Retrieved from: http://www.thescoopng.com/2015/01/12/nwachukwu-egbunike-choose-sit-fence/

64. Tony Egbulefu, "The social media war that made the presidential election tick," *Leadership*, 5 April 2015. Retrieved from: http://allafrica.com/stories/201504061704.html

65. Opeyemi Agbaje, "Themes from the 2015 elections," *Nigerian Politics Online*, 1 January 2016. Retrieved from: http://nigeriapoliticsonline.com/themes-from-the-2015-elections/

66. Emmanuel Onwubiko, "Hate speech; social media and the 2015 election," Point Blank News, 27 January 2015. Retrieved from: http://pointblanknews.com/pbn/articles-opinions/hate-speech-social-media-2015-election/

67. Sherry Turkle, *Life on the screen: Identity in the age of the Internet.* New York: Simon & Schuster, 1995.

68. Kelly Bergstrom, *First Monday 16*, no. 8 (1 August 2011): 7.

69. Judith S. Donath, "Identity and deception in the virtual community," in *Communities in cyberspace,* edited by Marc A. Smith and Peter Kollock, 27 -58. London: Routledge, 1999.

70. Lincoln Dahlberg, "Computer–mediated communication and the public sphere: A critical analysis," *Journal of Computer Mediated–Communication* 7, no. 1, at http://jcmc.indiana.edu/vol7/issue1/dahlberg.html, accessed 7 August 2010.

71. Same as 68 above.

72. Kelly Bergstrom, "'Don't feed the troll': shutting down debate about community expectations on Reddit.com." *First Monday 16*, no. 8 (1 August 2011): 1.

73. Cambria E, Chandra P, Sharma A and Hussain A., "Do not feel the trolls," in *Proceedings of the 3rd International Workshop on Social Data on the Web* (SDoW2010), edited by Passant A, Breslin J, Fernandez S, Bojars U, Workshop at the 9th International Semantic Web Conference (ISWC2010) - ISWC 2010 Workshops Volume I: Shanghai, China, 8 November 2010, Aachen,

Germany: CEUR Workshop Proceedings. SDoW2010 Social Data on the Web: Workshop at the 9th International Semantic Web Conference, 8 November 2010, Shanghai, China.

74.   Ali Mehdi, "Social media mela: trolling 101," *The Express Tribune*, 15 July 2012. Retrieved from: tribune.com.pk/story/408467/social-media-mela-trolling-101/

75.   Benkler, Y, *"The wealth of networks: how social production transforms markets and freedom,"* New Haven and London: Yale University Press, 2006.

76.   Lolade Nwanze, "Satire is a necessary and vital part of free speech, says Anenih," The Guardian, 16 November 2017. Retrieved from: https://guardian.ng/interview/satire-is-a-necessary-and-vital-part-of-free-speech-says-anenih/

77.   Papadonkee, "Abuja Politics: if a troll be washed away by the sea, the cabal is the less," *Abuja Politics*, 18 March 2017. Retrieved from: http://abujapolitics.blogspot.com/2017/03/if-troll-be-washed-away-by-sea-cabal-is.html

78.   Yemi Adesanya, "The Internet of Trolls: #TrollCabal and the Civic Commons," Nigerians Talk, 6 April 2017. Retrieved from: https://nigerianstalk.org/2017/04/06/the-internet-of-trolls-troll-cabal-and-the-civic-commons/

79.   Charles Ess, "The embodied self in a digital age: possibilities, risks, and prospects for a pluralistic (democratic/liberal) future?" *Nordicom Review*, no. 31 (January 2010):105-118.

80.   Same as 66 above.

81.   Kelly Bergstrom, "'Don't feed the troll': shutting down debate about community expectations on Reddit.com." *First Monday 16*, no. 8 (1 August 2011): 109.

82.   Yemi Adesanya, "The Internet of Trolls: #TrollCabal and the Civic Commons," Nigerians Talk, 6 April 2017. Retrieved from: https://nigerianstalk.org/2017/04/06/the-internet-of-trolls-troll-cabal-and-the-civic-commons/

83.   Peter Bradshaw, "Innocence of Muslims: a dark demonstration of the power of film," *The Guardian*, 17 September 2012. Retrieved from: https://www.theguardian.com/film/filmblog/2012/sep/17/innocence-of-muslims-demonstration-film.

84.   Scott Sayare and Nicola Clark, "French magazine runs cartoons that mock Muhammad," *The New York Times*, 19 September 2012. Retrieved from: https://www.nytimes.com/2012/09/20/world/europe/french-magazine-publishes-cartoons-mocking-muhammad.html

85.   Jidaw System, 22 Sept 2008. Retrieved from: http://www.jidaw.com/security/aisa/cybercrime_measures_nigeria.html

86.   The Paradigm, "#7YearsInJail Bill: Sen. Sefiu Kaka apologizes, promise to expunge controversial clause," 5 December 2013. Retrieved from: http://www.theparadigmng.com/2013/12/05/7yearsinjail-bill-sen-sefiu-kaka-apologizes-promise-to-expunge-controversial-clause/#

87.   An Act to provide for the prohibition of electronic fraud in all electronic transactions in Nigeria and for other related matters (SB198, Year: 2008)

88.   *Ibid*.

89.   *Ibid*

90.   Cybercrime Bill, 2013. Retrieved from: https://www.pinigeria. org/download/cybercrimebill2013.pdf

91.   E-mail interview that Gbenga Sesan granted to Nwachukwu Egbunike and Ellery Roberts Bridle on 9 December 2013.

92.   Nwachukwu Egbunike, "Nigeria: Senate President Calls for Social Media Censorship," *Global Voices*, 30 July 2012. Retrieved from: https://globalvoices.org/2012/07/30/nigeria-senate-president-calls-for-censorship-of-social-media/

93.   Nwachukwu Egbunike and Dominic Burbidge, "Nigerian government to ramp up internet surveillance?" *Global Voices Advocacy*, 12 July 2013. Retrieved from: https://advox.globalvoices. org/2013/07/12/nigerian-government-to-ramp-up-internet-surveillance/

94.   "Journal from an Ethiopian Prison: Testimony of Befeqadu Hailu," *Advox*, 14 October 2014. Retrieved on: https://advox. globalvoices.org/2014/10/14/journal-from-an-ethiopian-prison-testimony-of-befeqadu-hailu-part-1/

95.   Federal Negarit Gazeta of the Federal Democratic Republic of Ethiopia. 15th Year, No. 57, Addis Ababa, 28 August 2009. Retrieved from: https://trialtrackerblog.files.wordpress. com/2014/06/anti-terrorism-procl.pdf

96.   "Full Translation of Zone9ers Charge Sheet." August 12, 2014. *Trial Tracker Blog* (Reports on the trials of the jailed Zone 9 Bloggers in Ethiopia). Retrieved from: https://trialtrackerblog. org/2014/08/12/full-translation-of-zone9ers-charge-sheet/

97. *About Global Voices*. Retrieved from: https://globalvoices.org/about/

98. *About Advox*. Retrieved from: https://advox.globalvoices.org/about/

99. "STATEMENT: Global Voices Calls for the Release of Nine Journalists in Ethiopia," *Global Voices*, 2 May 2014. Retrieved from: https://advox.globalvoices.org/2014/05/02/statement-global-voices-calls-for-the-release-of-nine-journalists-in-ethiopia

100. Ellery Roberts Bridle, "#FreeZone9Bloggers: A Tweetathon Demanding the Release of Jailed Ethiopian Bloggers," *Global Voices Advocacy*, 12 May 2014. Retrieved from: https://advox.globalvoices.org/2014/05/12/join-the-freezone9bloggers-tweetathon-on-may-14/

101. Nwachukwu Egbunike, "Nigerian Blogger Blossom Nnodim Talks 'Social Media for Social Good,'" *Global Voices*, 6 February 2014. Retrieved from: https://globalvoices.org/2014/02/06/nigerian-blogger-blossom-nnodim-talks-social-media-for-social-good/#

102. Ellery Roberts Bridle, "From the [Four] Compass Points of the Earth Arises a Mighty Cry—#FreeZone9Bloggers!" *Global Voices Advocacy*, 4 August 2014. Retrieved from: https://advox.globalvoices.org/2014/08/04/from-the-four-compass-points-of-the-earth-arises-a-mighty-cry-freezone9bloggers/

103. Ellery Roberts Bridle, "Ethiopia: #FreeZone9Bloggers Trending on Tumblr," *Global Voices*, 19 May 2014. Retrieved from: https://globalvoices.org/2014/05/19/ethiopia-freezone9bloggers-trending-on-tumblr/, Ginio Gagliardone and Matti Pohjonen, "Engaging in Polarised Society: Social Media and Political Discourse

in Ethiopia," in Digital Activism in the Social Media Era, edited by B. Mustaviro. Palgrave Macmillan; 1st ed. 2016 edition (12 November 2016). DOI: 10.1007/978-3-319-40949-8_2

104. Ellery Roberts Bridle, "Five Ethiopian Journalists Freed from Prison, but Others Remain Behind Bars," *Global Voices Advocacy*, 8 July 2015. Retrieved from: https://advox.globalvoices.org/2015/07/09/breaking-three-ethiopian-journalists-freed-from-prison-but-others-remain-behind-bars/

105. AFP, "Ethiopia drops charges against Zone9 bloggers," 2015. Retrieved from: https://www.news24.com/Africa/News/ethiopia-drops-charges-against-zone-9-bloggers-20180214

Nwachukwu Egbunike lives in Ibadan, Nigeria. He holds a bachelor's degree in Medical Laboratory Sciences (specialising in Haematology and Medical Microbiology) from the University of Nigeria. He has two master's degrees in Communication from the University of Ibadan. His PhD research agenda is on social media and youth political participation. Egbunike is the author of a collection of socio-political critical essays entitled *Dyed Thoughts: A Conversation in and from my Country* (2012). His book, *Blazing Moon* was the 2nd place winner of the Association of Nigerian Authors 2015 Prize in Poetry.